PARABLES

Parables:
Putting Jesus's Stories in Their Place

Parables

978-1-7910-3505-1

978-1-7910-3506-8 *eBook*

Parables DVD

978-1-7910-3509-9

Parables Leader Guide

978-1-7910-3507-5

978-1-7910-3508-2 *eBook*

Also by Josh Scott:

Bible Stories for Grown-Ups:
Reading Scripture with New Eyes

Context: Putting Scripture in Its Place

Josh Scott

PARABLES

Putting Jesus's Stories in Their Place

Abingdon Press | Nashville

Parables

Putting Jesus's Stories in Their Place

Copyright © 2025 Abingdon Press
All rights reserved.

Library of Congress Control Number: 2024948571
978-1-7910-3505-1

MANUFACTURED IN THE
UNITED STATES OF AMERICA

For The Scott Crew
Carla, Cohen, Jaylyn, Jasmine, Ava, and Colton
Thank you for always loving and supporting me.
My super love you.

CONTENTS

INTRODUCTION

A "FOR INSTANCE"

A few months back I had a conversation with my oldest son that stopped me in my tracks. Parenting is full of these moments that catch us off guard, especially when kids reach their teenage years. However, the surprising moment wasn't related to anything he said to me, but something that I said to him. Perhaps a little background would help here.

When I was a teenager, my dad used a certain phrase that would absolutely drive me up the wall. When he'd talk to me about my behavior or grades or driving—anything about which I needed to adjust my attitude, really—he would say, "Let me give you a 'for instance.'" This was usually the moment in the conversation where I knew we'd be there for a while and, simultaneously, I began to regret whatever choices I had made that put us here. Those seven words were followed by a story he would concoct to help me learn a particular lesson.

"Let me give you a 'for instance,'" he'd say to his son who dreamed of pitching at the major league level. "Imagine there's a kid who wanted to pitch in the majors, and he spent all his time, hours and hours, working on his pitches, but didn't study at all. If his grades dropped, what would happen?"

Point received, Dad. Looking back, I realize that his "for instances" were trying to elicit my participation in learning. A "for instance" was intended to expand my imagination and convey something meaningful by making me part of the learning process. I get that now, but decades later I can still remember how hard I had to work to keep my eyes from rolling. It's one of those "dad phrases" that I swore to myself I would never use on my kids.

Back to that recent conversation with my own teenager, who is so much like his father. I can't remember what we were talking about, but I can tell you that I knew I wasn't conveying the point I was making very well. Grasping at straws, I opened my mouth and the words escaped before I even knew what happened: "Let me give you a 'for instance.' Imagine there's a kid who wanted to play in the NBA, and he spent all his time working on his shooting and rebounding, but didn't study at all. If his grades dropped, what would happen?"

I couldn't believe what I'd just said. It was as if someone else was speaking for me. I kid you not, those words weren't even in my head. They were an unconscious response from somewhere deep in the recesses of my memory. It was as if my dad had momentarily possessed my body and was parenting through me. As you might imagine, my son seemed to find the phrase just as compelling, and appreciated it just as much, as I did at his age. Needless to say, I now have a much greater appreciation for what my dad was attempting to do. Parenting is tough, and I realize now that Chip Scott knew way more about life than I gave him credit for when I was sixteen.

The years have also helped me to better understand why he went for a story as the go-to method of explaining important things. Stories have a unique power. They have the capacity to disarm us, challenge us, shape us, and inspire us. The best stories can cause us to rethink and even change our minds about important things. That's exactly what my dad was hoping for when he gave me a "for instance." I guess it's what I was also hoping for when I accidentally said those same words to my own son.

The power of story is not a modern phenomenon. Before humans could read or write, we were storytelling creatures. Through our stories we passed down myth and meaning. They connected and connect us to the past and hold our dreams for the future. To put it simply, stories are deeply interconnected with what it means to be human. It should not surprise us, then, that the Bible is filled with stories and storytellers.

Jesus of Nazareth is known for many things. He was a healer, a worker of wonders, a teacher of wisdom, and a prophet. Perhaps one of the things about him most familiar to us is that he was a gifted storyteller. His stories, called *parables*, are his version of a "for instance." In response to questions, accusations, misunderstandings, and controversies Jesus most often responded not with a lecture or sermon but with a story.

In Luke 10, a legal expert asked Jesus, "Who is my neighbor?" An important question, to which Jesus replied by telling the story we know as "the good Samaritan." "For instance: A man was going down from Jerusalem to Jericho and fell into the hands of robbers."

Later, in Luke 15, when Jesus was criticized for eating with "tax collectors and sinners," he responded with a trilogy of "for instance" stories:

"Which one of you, having a hundred sheep and losing one of them, does not leave the ninety-nine in the wilderness and go after the one that is lost until he finds it?"
(Luke 15:4)

"Or what woman having ten silver coins, if she loses one of them, does not light a lamp, sweep the house, and search carefully until she finds it?"
(Luke 15:8)

"There was a man who had two sons. The younger of them said to his father, 'Father, give me the share of the wealth that will belong to me.' So he divided his assets between them."

(Luke 15:11-12)

These examples just begin to scratch the surface. Telling stories, parables, was a central facet of Jesus's approach to sharing his message and vision. In fact, at least one-third of Jesus's teaching in the Synoptic Gospels (a term that means "seeing together," and describes the relationship between Mark, Matthew, and Luke) involved parables. According to Mark's Gospel, parables were Jesus's primary method of communication with the crowds: "With many such parables he [Jesus] spoke the word to them as they were able to hear it; he did not speak to them except in parables, but he explained everything in private to his disciples" (Mark 4:33-34).

Telling stories, parables, was a central facet of Jesus's approach to sharing his message and vision.

In this study we will focus on six of Jesus's parables, three that are grounded in the everyday experience of domestic life (wine-making, gardening, and baking) and three that are centered in the social and economic experience and tension that his audience would have known in their bones (tenant farmers, day laborers, and a party/feast). Our task is to explore how these stories spoke then, in Jesus's day, and how they still speak today, sometimes in very surprising ways. Before we begin that exploration, however, let's first talk about what parables are and how they functioned in Jesus's teaching.

SIDE BY SIDE

The word *parable, parabolē* in Greek, means "to cast alongside." A parable is a kind of creative juxtaposition that places two things next to each other, side by side, for the purpose of either drawing a comparison or making a contrast, or both. At their core, parables are stories. They have a plot, a narrative, characters, and some kind of action. In a parable something happens and that happening has significant implications:

+ Someone went out and sowed some seeds, and they fell on different kinds of soil. Some of the seed produced and some did not.
+ A man went on a journey and entrusted his property to his servants. Eventually, he came back to settle up the accounts.
+ A rich man had a bumper crop and built bigger barns to store it, but he didn't share his abundance with his neighbors. He died instead of getting to enjoy his jam-packed barns.

Parables are stories, but they aren't *just* stories. Their primary goal is not entertainment, or even just explaining a moral about how to live or what to believe. Instead, like good stories and good storytellers, parables include their audience in the process. What we have in the Gospels are likely summations of Jesus's parables, a concentrated synopsis that gives us the gist of the story. In reality Jesus probably told at least some of these stories several times, and the content and shape likely varied depending on the audience and how they were responding. This is an experience I have become all too familiar with as a pastor.

When I preach a sermon, I come with some notes that keep me focused on the overall structure and point of the message, but when

I deliver it more than once, the two versions are not identical. Based on how the room is responding I might spend more or less time in a particular area, think of a different story to help make a point, or create different lighthearted moments. The essence of the sermons will be the same, but the two sermons will have their own unique twists based on the audience. Imagine a crowd responding to a story like that of the good Samaritan, and Jesus really building the tension and the drama, for example. Good storytellers, like Jesus, weren't just repeating details; they were working with the crowd, piquing their interest to draw their attention more deeply into the meaning of the story. Part of a parable's power is that they are participatory events. They invite listeners to engage, to enter the world of the story, and to ask what it means and what their response should be.

CALLING US HERE AND NOW

The point of Jesus's parables was to announce the kingdom of God, not as a future place that could be experienced when we abandon this world, but as a present and available reality that we can taste and see, here and now. Another way of thinking about the kingdom of God, if that language is too antiquated, is that it represents God's dream for the world. What would the world be like, the parables ask, if God's dream of justice and enough-ness for everyone came true? Parables press even further to ask something of us: What role can we play in making that dream a reality?

As you might imagine, some of Jesus's first listeners found the idea of the kingdom/dream of God as present possibility a bit naive. After all, he's announcing the here-and-now-ness of God's kingdom under the oppression and occupation of the Roman Empire. How can God's dream be fulfilled, and how can the Kingdom have come when the facts of the ground don't seem to reflect that reality. We'll see this tension in the parables we explore together.

The creative genius of Jesus's parables is that they begin with a premise that would have been mundanely, or even infuriatingly, familiar to his audience. A farmer sowing seed, or tenant farmers and day laborers harvesting grapes, become vehicles through which the unfamiliar and unexpected can be introduced and explained. The everydayness of wine-making, mustard seeds, baking bread, and the real-life experiences of workers being treated unjustly become the avenues through which Jesus describes the nature of God's kingdom. For Jesus, God's kingdom was not an otherworldly possibility at the end of time, but the prospect of a more just and equitable world, now.

HEAVENLY STORIES, EARTHLY MEANINGS

Jesus's parables are often described as "earthly stories with heavenly meanings," but I find that phrase to be unhelpful. It can be interpreted in ways that suggest the parables of Jesus are drawing our attention away from the world of the present and into the future of heaven. That is just not the case. If anything, Jesus's parables are heavenly stories with earthly meanings. By "heavenly" I mean that they are stories about God and God's kingdom. Think of the way we similarly say "the White House" or "Washington" when referring to the president or their administration. In these stories Jesus talks about the dream of God for the world, how heaven would reorder the earth with justice and compassion. Put another way, parables illuminate the gap between the way things currently were/are and God's justice. How would God's kingdom transform a world of injustice, violence, and inequality? Jesus's parables offer that vision and possibility.

With this in mind, it's paramount we remember that Jesus told these stories in a first-century Jewish context, and not a twenty-first-century American one. To hear his message, we will necessarily have to talk about the world of social and economic pressures that impacted the kinds of stories he told. If we approach these stories from our modern lenses first, we will be more likely to force our interpretations to align with our context and values and miss the challenge Jesus's parables deliver. Grounding these stories in their first-century political, social, and economic context will be essential for hearing their message, then, and discerning how to apply them today.

Jesus's parables are meant to disturb, challenge, and convict us.

Jesus's parables are meant to disturb, challenge, and convict us. They are also invitations to think differently, embrace new possibilities, and participate in the making of a new world. Admittedly, in my first decades of life and ministry this understanding of parables was absent from my engagement with Jesus's stories. I have learned that this is not a unique experience, but one that is shared and all too common. Jesus's parables have an edge, and over time some of the discomfort they bring has been obscured and blunted by approaches to interpretation that import our cultural values into the world of Jesus's stories. By doing this we have transformed many of Jesus's challenges of unjust situations into affirmations of the very actions and systems he intended to critique. Much of our work in the pages ahead is focused on putting Jesus's stories in their place by taking seriously the world in which he told them. Once we hear them in their own context, their meaning for us will become more accessible.

In this study I will offer some interpretations that may not be familiar. This is not because I have decided that I just don't like the conventional interpretations and want to offer something else that is more palatable. I do this because some of the ways we have been taught to read and interpret Jesus's stories have failed to take into account the context in which he lived and the vision of God that inspired his mission. Whether you go with me fully or not, I hope what I offer in the pages ahead will be interesting, inspire curiosity, and offer practical application that bridges Jesus's world and ours.

The point of a parable, after all, is not to be lost in another world but to inspire action in this one. Jesus doesn't dabble in theory. He tells stories we can taste and smell—about wine, mustard, and bread—and stories whose plot and characters described the world his first listeners would have recognized as their own. His stories named and critiqued the status quo, and, at the same time, created possible alternatives that could be realized if we join God and one another to make them reality. That's also the goal of this book, to invite us to hear Jesus's challenge in hopes that we will be empowered to participate in the making of a more just, generous, and compassionate world.

THREE ASKS

Before we begin, I have three asks of you, my readers. This study will examine six of Jesus's parables, most of which will likely be somewhat familiar, and that familiarity can present an interpretive impediment. When we are familiar with something, when we know it so well that we approach it with assumption and not curiosity, we can actually become unfamiliar with it. If I bring any assumption with me to the Bible, I want it to be the assumption that, no matter how much I have read or studied a particular text, there are still surprises left to be discovered. With that in mind, my first ask is that you join me in coming to these stories with an open mind and open heart. Bring your curiosity and your questions. Let's try to hear these stories afresh, as if for the very first time. If we do that, if we can engage Jesus's parables in their context and not import into them the interpretations and assumptions we've inherited, I am confident there are "aha!" moments that await us in the pages ahead.

My second ask is that we sit with the discomfort and challenge of these stories when we don't know what else to do. The preeminent historical Jesus scholar of our day, John Dominic Crossan, has aptly noted the way parables can affect us: "You can usually recognize a parable," he says, "because your immediate reaction will be self-contradictory:'I don't know what you mean by that story but I'm certain I don't like it.'"[1] No doubt we will experience this tension more than once as we move ahead. As I have worked with the parables over the years there have been times that, when surprised with something new that I didn't quite know what to do with, I had to just sit in the tension of what Jesus seemed to be saying and how my own life was out of balance with it. We can acknowledge that tension and disjointedness, and also not rush to an answer or resolution. Jesus's understanding of the Kingdom was not as a sprint but a marathon. It takes time, like a planted seed becoming a blossoming plant. Our responsibility is to show up with openness, patience, and a watering can.

Finally, I ask that we remember that, while this is a book about stories, it's not just about stories. Jesus's parables are fiction about nonfiction. They are narratives created to describe the concrete reality of his audience and to also engage their imagination about what their world could be if God's will was done on earth as it is in heaven. Additionally, these stories will challenge us to think about more than characters and plot but will also ask us to reflect on the important beliefs we hold. Jesus's parables will lead us to think about how we understand God's character and how that impacts the way we live and move in the world. That is maybe the most interesting feature of Jesus's stories: They are not monologues, but dialogues. They do not preach to us or at us as much as they invite us into a conversation about how things are and how they could be. Parables don't really answer our questions; instead, they ask questions of us. To read and reflect on a parable is to enter into a conversation with the parable-teller, Jesus himself, and with one another as we attempt to hear and respond to the challenge they present. That conversation begins now.

CHAPTER 1

Wine and Wineskins

VOLCANOES AND FERMENTATION

My fifth-grade year wasn't super memorable. I'm hard pressed to remember who was in my class or what field trip we took that year. There is one particular event, however, that is burned deep into my memory. It involved a volcano and a kid who didn't like to wait for instructions. That kid was me.

Our teacher, Mrs. Borders, had asked us to bring in a few supplies for a science experiment. I loved science experiments. Not because I learned a lot from them, mind you. I wasn't what you would call a motivated student. I loved them because they were an interruption to the day in, day out monotony of school. It was a chance to do something, to expend a little of the frenetic energy that was bottled up in my ten-year-old body. It was that same energy that got me in trouble on that fateful day.

The experiment was to create a volcano by combining baking soda and vinegar in a mason jar in order to observe the reaction between the two substances. As you probably know, when the vinegar, an acid, is combined with the baking soda, a carbonate, the ensuing chemical reaction causes the release of carbon dioxide, which makes the volcano "erupt." Simple enough, right? Not so fast.

After we all got our supplies ready, while the teacher gave us our instructions, I went ahead and dumped the vinegar into the jar. As soon as I did, Mrs. Borders said, "Don't do anything yet. We'll all pour our vinegar in at the same time."

I immediately put both of my hands on top of the glass jar to prevent the evidence of my failure to listen to her directions from spilling all over the floor. Unfortunately, she saw me and knew something was up. She came over and asked me to move my hands away from the jar.

"You don't want me to do that," I said.

"Yes, I do," she replied. "Move your hands so I can see what you've done."

I had no other option, so I quickly removed my hands. What I didn't realize is that the whole time the chemical reaction I was attempting to restrain had been building pressure in the mason jar. The glass didn't give, and the pressure needed to go somewhere, and go somewhere it did. As soon as I moved my hands the contents of the jar exploded. What happened next is the stuff of legend. I don't know that anyone could give an accurate description of the aftermath. Very quickly the story had by accretion of imagination grown into something larger than life.

Some said the contents went so high that a ceiling tile was dislodged. To be fair, the ceiling was pretty low. Others said the teacher, bending over to look into the jar, had her glasses knocked off when she was caught in the blast. The one thing I am sure of is that I went immediately to see the principal to discuss the situation.

Believe it or not, I think about that story every time I hear a short parable Jesus tells in each of the Synoptic Gospels. He describes his activity using the image of new wine being poured into an old wineskin and the latter's capacity to contain the contents entrusted to it. If this is a familiar image for us, we might be tempted to assume the point of this short but significant parable is fairly obvious: Jesus is doing something new, specifically, making a break with Judaism and founding a new religion, Christianity. My encouragement as we explore this (or any other) parable is for us to attempt, as best we can, to bracket our assumptions and the interpretations we've previously heard, and to give these stories fresh hearings. So before we rush to interpretation by assigning meaning to these two symbols—the wine and the wineskin—let's step back and examine the larger context in which this saying occurs.

ONE TEXT, MULTIPLE VOICES

First, let's look at the text of the parable itself. As I mentioned, this parable is included by Mark, Matthew, and Luke, and each of the authors situates the saying in similar contexts in their stories. The sayings in Mark and Matthew are similar, a different word or two, but essentially the same content.

> "No one sews a piece of unshrunk cloth on an old cloak; otherwise, the patch pulls away from it, the new from the old, and a worse tear is made. Similarly, no one puts new wine into old wineskins; otherwise, the wine will burst the skins, and the wine is lost, and so are the skins, but one puts new wine into fresh wineskins."
>
> (Mark 2:21-22)

> "No one sews a piece of unshrunk cloth on an old cloak, for the patch pulls away from the cloak, and a worse tear is made. Neither is new wine put into old wineskins; otherwise, the skins burst, and the wine is spilled, and

the skins are ruined, but new wine is put into fresh wineskins, and so both are preserved."

(*Matthew 9:16-17*)

Luke shares the same basic content, but at the end there is a statement that seems to directly contradict what Jesus says. It is also in Luke's version that this doublet about cloths and wineskins is called "parable."

He also told them a parable: "No one tears a piece from a new garment and sews it on an old garment; otherwise, not only will one tear the new garment, but the piece from the new will not match the old garment. Similarly, no one puts new wine into old wineskins; otherwise, the new wine will burst the skins and will spill out, and the skins will be ruined. But new wine must be put into fresh wineskins. And no one after drinking old wine desires new wine but says, 'The old is good.'"

(*Luke 5:36-39*)

As you can see, Luke has the same contrast between something new and something old, but then, at the end, there's an added line that undermines the very core of Jesus's teaching. After explaining his work (we'll learn more about why he's doing this soon) with the image of new, fermenting wine, Luke adds the additional line, verse 39, a kind of addendum about people preferring the old wine over the new. There are a couple reasons that this might be the case. One suggestion is that this is an addition to the text, perhaps added later by a scribe or copyist. Some ancient manuscripts lack verse 39. Maybe they were uncomfortable with how this text was being interpreted, and they wanted to make sure the old was not demonized by the advent of the new. I'll have more to say on this soon. A second suggestion is that Luke is offering a concession or reflecting the reality that there were those who did not welcome the particular kind of new that Jesus was attempting to bring. Both seem like plausible explanations for me, and since we end up engaging the text as it has come down to us, both explanations can be illuminating and helpful.

Next, we turn to the context in which this parable occurs. It is essentially the same in all three of these Gospels. The parable about new cloth and wine in the Synoptic Gospels is not a random, disconnected saying, like in Thomas. It is used to explain Jesus's activity, which was beginning to stir up controversy. Moving forward, since the context is similar (Matthew does follow this episode with a different story than those found in Mark and Luke, but it doesn't alter the meaning of the parable), I will use the text from Mark.

TO FAST OR
NOT TO FAST?

When we meet Jesus in Mark, he's not wrapped in swaddling clothes and lying in a manger. He comes on the scene as an adult to be baptized by John in the Jordan River. This was followed immediately with a forty-day period of temptation in the wilderness, the details of which were not narrated until Matthew wrote his version. When the news broke of John's imprisonment by Antipas, Jesus must have experienced it as a catalyst for his own movement. He went to Galilee and began announcing what he called "good news": "The time is fulfilled, and the kingdom of God has come near" (1:15). This wasn't just a movement of words, however. Jesus also began to enact his vision of God's kingdom in ways that generated controversy: he healed the sick, exorcised unclean spirits, and ate scandalous meals. That last one, eating, is at the center of understanding the parable of the new wine.

As we arrive in Mark 2, the controversy brewing centers on Jesus's disciples and their approach, or lack thereof, to fasting. In the Jewish tradition, fasting was done collectively on holy days like Yom Kippur (the Day of Atonement) and Tisha B'Av (the date that commemorates disasters such as the destruction of both the First and Second Temples), but it was also engaged in at other times as a form of spiritual practice. Fasting was about contrition and repentance, as we see, for example, in the story of Jonah. When the king of Nineveh heard that the great city was going to be destroyed, he declared that neither human nor animal should eat or drink anything as part of demonstrating their changed ways.

Fasting was about contrition and repentance, as we see, for example, in the story of Jonah.

The Pharisees had a set rhythm of fasting twice per week, on Monday and Thursday. And it really is no surprise that John's disciples were fasting. He seems to have developed the reputation in the Gospels of being a bit of a killjoy. When Jesus contrasted his ministry with that of John's he put it like this:

> "For John came neither eating nor drinking, and they say, 'He has a demon'; the Son of Man came eating and drinking, and they say, 'Look, a glutton and a drunkard, a friend of tax collectors and sinners!'"
>
> (Matthew 11:18-19)

John was an ascetic who practiced self-denial and lived minimally—he stayed in the desert, didn't wear fine clothes, and when he did eat, it was locusts and honey. John probably wasn't getting many invites to dinner, but I think that was fine by him. He didn't have time

for small talk. He was awaiting what he believed would be God's immanent intervention to set the world right. At any moment, John believed,
God would break into the world and even the score. His images were
vivid, his warnings urgent.

> But when he saw many of the Pharisees and Sadducees coming for
> his baptism, he said to them, "You brood of vipers! Who warned
> you to flee from the coming wrath? Therefore, bear fruit worthy of
> repentance, and do not presume to say to yourselves, 'We have Abraham
> as our ancestor,' for I tell you, God is able from these stones to raise up
> children to Abraham. Even now the ax is lying at the root of the trees;
> therefore every tree that does not bear good fruit will be cut down and
> thrown into the fire."
>
> (Matthew 3:7-10)

When you are convinced you are living at a tipping point, like John
was, the idea of having a nice house, fashionable clothes, and lavish din-
ners don't make sense. You have too much work to do to make sure you
and those around you are prepared for, and on the right side of, God's
intervention.

The Pharisees and John's disciples, at least based on John's preaching, were not what you'd call "allies." Yet here they were, suddenly
finding themselves on common ground. The Pharisees came to Jesus,
frustrated that his disciples were not fasting like they were, in prepara-
tion for God's deliverance. In fact, they were doing quite the opposite—
celebrating like it had already happened. In the story that immediately
precedes the fasting controversy, Jesus had called a tax collector named
Levi to leave his collection booth and follow him instead. Immediately,
Levi did just that; he bailed mid-shift and invited Jesus into his home.
The next scene opens with Jesus and his disciples sitting with Levi and
other "sinners" feasting. I like to imagine music and laughter filling the

air and spilling out of Levi's house. How could the neighbors not notice with all that commotion?

Jesus's presence in the home of a tax collector must have felt like a betrayal to those watching from the larger community. Tax collectors were collaborators with the Roman occupiers. They enriched themselves at the expense of the surrounding community. Knowing that, can't we empathize and understand why some of the Pharisees observing Jesus's action might have bristled and questioned his decision to feast at the home of a traitor like Levi? It is not borne out of the caricature of legalistic Judaism that many of us inherited. It's a frustration that what Jesus is doing seems to ignore, in their minds, the problems created by the Levis of the world.

When asked about this glaring difference in approach, feasting instead of fasting, Jesus's response was that "to fast or not to fast" is not the question. Jesus understands it as a question about timing. Before he offers the parable of the new wine, Jesus first explains his disciples' lack of fasting with the image of a wedding celebration.

> Jesus said to them, "The wedding attendants cannot fast while the bridegroom is with them, can they? As long as they have the bridegroom with them, they cannot fast. The days will come when the bridegroom is taken away from them, and then they will fast on that day."
>
> (Mark 2:19-20)

Notice, first, that Jesus does not condemn the Pharisees or John's disciple for fasting, nor does he label it something legalistic that is meant to be left behind. He even indicates that his disciples will eventually fast when "the bridegroom is taken away from them." In the present moment, however, the bridegroom is present and that requires feasting, not fasting. For us, this might seem to be a strange metaphor to use, but Jesus's listeners would have understood the significance of the wedding scenario immediately.

When the Hebrew prophets envisioned the future, they imagined that one day God would put things right in the world. On that day, the *Day of the Lord*, justice would roll like waters. God would deal with Israel's oppressors, bringing liberation and freedom to a people who had known the weight of living under one empire after another for generations. They were imagining an end and a beginning. The end of the present age, full of injustice, and the beginning of the age to come, which was grounded in God's concern for a just and equitable world. What that would ultimately look like varied from prophet to prophet, because they all didn't share the same vision of that future and who would be included. For some, those with a nationalist bent, that future would only include Israel. That was bad news for the other nations of the world. For others, however, there was a more universal vision of the future, one in which the nations streamed to Israel to worship God. One of the common images or metaphors for that Day of the Lord was that of a wedding celebration, a feast that would be the indicator that the old age was gone, and a new one had dawned—a world that was transformed from a place of injustice and violence to a place marked by justice and peace. Notice how Isaiah imagines the scene:

> On this mountain the LORD of hosts will make for all peoples
> a feast of rich food, a feast of well-aged wines,
> of rich food filled with marrow, of well-aged wines strained clear.
> And he will destroy on this mountain
> the shroud that is cast over all peoples,
> the covering that is spread over all nations;
> he will swallow up death forever.
> Then the Lord GOD will wipe away the tears from all faces,
> and the disgrace of his people he will take away from all the earth,
> for the LORD has spoken.
> It will be said on that day,

> *"See, this is our God; we have waited for him, so that he might save us.*
>
> *This is the LORD for whom we have waited;*
>
> *let us be glad and rejoice in his salvation."*
>
> For the hand of the LORD will rest on this mountain.
>
> *(Isaiah 25:6-10a)*

To understand Jesus's metaphor and action we have to understand what time it was. He wasn't anti-fasting. He was convinced that he was living at the end of one age and, through his movement, ushering in that promised age to come. This wasn't about the *end of the world* as we have often misunderstood it. This was about *the end of the world as they knew it.* Jesus was not—at least I don't think—imagining that life on earth was coming to an end. He was convicted that God was acting to do what the prophets had foretold. In that way, Jesus and John had a similar perspective. They were both living at the end of the age. The key difference was found in *how* that new age would be born.

GOD IS LOOKING FOR PARTNERS

As we saw, John believed in God's immanent intervention. He called his listeners to prepare by repentance, and as we've seen, a little fasting can go a long way in that process. Yet after John's imprisonment, Jesus launched a movement centered on the kingdom of God that had significant differences from John's. First, John's message was about the future. Someday soon God would act. Jesus's message announced that the time had come; the Kingdom was already here and accessible. Second, John's message focused on God's intervention. God would do the acting; they would enjoy the benefit. For Jesus, everything about his message and movement was grounded in an understanding that God would act in history through human participation. That's why Jesus was going around healing and liberating people. It was a sign that the Kingdom was not coming someday but was already here and now. That's why Jesus was feasting with tax collectors. But the moment Levi abandoned his post and (like Zacchaeus in Luke's Gospel, I'm sure) stopped harming his community, the Kingdom *was present already*, not in a future moment of divine intervention, but in the present moment of human and divine partnership. Levi had stopped collaborating with the empire and started collaborating with God. One age was dying, and another being born. Feasting is the only response to that good news. When Jesus used that wedding feast imagery, his audience (and Mark's) would have readily understood the metaphor being engaged.

However, Jesus's disciples will eventually fast, when he, the bridegroom, is taken from them. This is no doubt a messianic allusion, and one that points toward the eventual confrontation between two drastically different visions for the world: Rome's vision of empire and Jesus's vision of God's kingdom. The collision course is set and foreshadowed. Finally, Jesus starts talking about patching garments and making wine.

A NEW WINE
FOR A NEW WORLD

The standard commentary on this parable often pits Jesus and his movement over and against his Jewish roots. The new wine, it's suggested, is the new religion Jesus was starting: Christianity. The old wineskin that couldn't contain it was Judaism. It seems obvious, right? Simply put, Jesus never stopped being Jewish, and he never started a new religion. Judaism was the religion *of* Jesus, and Christianity is a religion that eventually began *about* Jesus. We must stop setting Jesus up as an enemy of his own tradition. Whatever Jesus meant by the wine and wineskin metaphor, he didn't mean that.

We must stop setting Jesus up as an enemy of his own tradition.

Perhaps spending a moment with the science of the parable might give us some insight into what Jesus is up to with these images. On the surface, especially if we aren't familiar with the processes of winemaking, this might seem to be a strange metaphor. However, it's a similar process to the volcano experiment I described at the beginning of the chapter. Just like the vinegar and baking soda react to make the "eruption," in the fermentation process it is yeast breaking down carbohydrates that creates a chemical reaction. The culmination of that event creates two things: alcohol and carbon dioxide. More on that in a moment.

Wine is made in a couple of stages. There is the stage we might call "primary fermentation," when the yeast begins to break down the sugars in the grape juice. After that, there is a further stage that can last days, weeks, months, or even years. This is when the alcohol levels rise and, because fermentation is still happening, gas is released. Here we begin to understand the metaphor with which Jesus is playing. A wineskin was made of the leathered skin of an animal—usually a sheep or goat. When the wineskins were new, they were flexible. They had the capacity to expand with the fermenting wine contained within them. However, with time they lost that capacity and became inflexible, rigid. When that time came, the wineskin could no longer contain the fermentation process, as the contents grew and pressed against its unmalleable boundaries. It would swell and burst, spilling the wine everywhere.

The question for us is, If Jesus isn't talking about starting a new religion, what is he doing with the new wine and wineskin imagery? As I mentioned in the introduction, Jesus's parables are not just clever stories that teach timeless truths. His primary use of the medium of storytelling was not just to teach us to be kind or to work hard, and so on. Parables occur at the intersection of the way the world works now and the kingdom of God. They create a comparison or contrast between how things are and how they could be. Jesus is doing just that with this parable.

Jesus's "new wine" was not about starting a new religion, but it was a call to his own tradition, and all traditions really, to be open to the ways the Spirit might surprise them. Perhaps the Spirit was fomenting—or in this case fermenting—a kind of chemical reaction that could transform life as Jesus's disciples knew it. When God's dream is coupled with human collaboration, new realities become possible. Because they were living at the intersection of the ages, and God's future was already being experienced, they could not operate under what had been accepted as "the way the world works." God's new age would not reinforce existing conditions; it would require a rethinking and reimagining of what was possible. That being the case, he calls his followers to remain flexible and expansive, ready to experience the possibilities of God's kingdom on earth, as it is in heaven.

Further, when Jesus talks about "new wine," he is referring to his vision of the kingdom of God. What was that vision and what was it like? We have already seen it: healing, liberating, feasting, and pulling in close those who've been kept at the margins. In Luke 4, Jesus is said to have quoted from the prophet Isaiah, chapter 61, during a sermon in his hometown of Nazareth:

> "*The Spirit of the Lord is upon me,*
> > *because he has anointed me*
> > > *to bring good news to the poor.*
> *He has sent me to proclaim release to the captives*
> > *and recovery of sight to the blind,*
> > > *to set free those who are oppressed,*
> *to proclaim the year of the Lord's favor."*
> > > > > > (Luke 4:18-19)

To put it succinctly, Jesus's vision of God's kingdom was that of a just, equitable, liberative, healing, nonviolent community. It was not confined to a future reality someday, but one that Jesus saw as present and available, advancing every time a tax collector left their post or someone who had been alienated was brought close. It was a radical departure from the structures, systems, and conventional wisdom that defined and determined the old age. That is why Jesus compares business as usual with an old wineskin. The system of empire cannot contain the new order Jesus envisions, because empire depends on inequality and violence to maintain its dominance.

We might make Jesus's point more obvious if we put it like this: you can't realize God's dream in Rome's system. Jesus was not advocating for a different kind of supremacy or inequality. The goal wasn't to use the system of empire except with a different theology animating it, because empire is empire, even with a more generous theology behind it. This parable is not a repudiation or rejection of Judaism, then, but a rejection of empire and violence as the inevitable way the world has to be and a call to participation and expansion of our hearts and imaginations.

NEW WINESKINS TODAY

One of the central questions we bring with us to any biblical text is, What about us, today? That's not a question we bring to other literature, is it? We don't read Shakespeare or Hemingway and try to find a way to apply it to our lives, but when it comes to Scripture, especially the red letters for Christians, we want to find resonance in our own experience. How might a parable that originated in a pushback against empire and the violence that upholds it be applied to our lives today? I have a few thoughts.

First, it seems the more things change, the more they stay the same. Jesus's followers have a long, tragic track record of trying to advance his vision in ways that contradict his values. Too many times we have been seduced by the empty promises of empire. While bearing the name of Jesus we have behaved in ways that are so painfully un-Christlike, launching crusades, inquisitions, and drawing sharp, deep boundaries to keep out those whose doctrinal purity doesn't check all our boxes. This is an especially important point in the United States today, as a growing number of Christians are embracing the idea of Christian nationalism. The temptation Jesus resisted when he refused to bring about God's kingdom without also committing to the values that come along with it is tripping us up. If we Christians had understood the depth of this parable, we might have avoided the violence and pursuit of Christian empire that has marked the last two thousand years and continues into the present. As Jesus says elsewhere, let those with ears hear.

Another meaning, in the first century and for the twenty-first century and beyond, calls our attention to the need for winemakers in every generation. Many of us have been taught, whether implicitly or explicitly, that pretty much everything that can be learned, said, or discovered has already happened. Sometime in the past, be it the first or fourth or sixteenth century, they (our spiritual ancestors) cracked the code, got the answers, and put them in a nice, neat system for us. Our job is to believe that, to repeat it, and to pass it on without messing it up. To be sure, there is a part of our faith tradition that is about learning from past discoveries. However, there is still new wine that needs to be made. The Spirit is still moving, we are still learning, and a natural result of that process is that we will change our minds on some things. That is what the word *repent* actually means, to change our minds.

Thankfully, we have seen this movement happen, albeit slowly and reluctantly at times, throughout our history. In the 1600s Galileo was labeled a heretic for, rightly, suggesting that the earth revolves around the sun, and not vice versa. That view did not match a literal reading of Scripture. It took the church until 1992 to officially clear his name. The same Bible that was used to condemn Galileo has also been used to defend slavery, racism, and white supremacy. Chapter and verse have been quoted to uphold patriarchy and misogyny, and to condemn and exclude the LGBTQ+ community from full participation in the life of the church—and that is just in the last couple hundred years. And, while we still have a very, very long way to go, winemakers have emerged in every generation to call our attention to the new-to-us wine the Spirit is fermenting. I say "new-to-us" because I am convinced that God isn't, generation after generation, realizing that these phobias, bigotries, and biases are wrong and dehumanizing. God hasn't been waiting for us to point out the problems. God has been waiting on us to move forward, to follow the Spirit deeper into ways of relating and being that create the potential for human flourishing for all of God's kids. We are always catching up, and we have more catching up to do.

No generation will figure it all out, of course. Our challenge is to do our part in our moment, to collaborate with the Spirit to ferment new wine for our time.

God hasn't been waiting for us to point out the problems. God has been waiting on us to move forward, to follow the Spirit deeper into ways of relating and being that create the potential for human flourishing for all of God's kids.

Finally, this parable calls us to remain open, flexible, and ready to expand. Jesus's use of this image of an old wineskin that cannot meet the moment and a fresh one that can grow to hold its contents was not intended to represent a one-off situation. Jesus wasn't saying, "Let's be flexible and expansive now, this one time, and after that we can go back to being rigid and immovable." It will take regular, attentive work for us to remain in a state of openness to growth. Thankfully, that is what religion at its best is all about. When religion devolved into an attempt to manufacture certainty (which we can't have), generate fear (which we don't need), or just prove how right *we* are and how wrong *they* are, it hasn't lived up to its purpose. Religion, faith, spirituality—whatever you want to call it—is about staying open. It isn't there to lull us to sleep, but to awaken us to the possibilities that are generated by Divine-human collaboration. Religion at its best piques our curiosity, inspires wonder, and keeps us limber and flexible.

What can we do to keep ourselves open? I have found regular practices that focus our attention and bring us into the moment are helpful. Reading Scripture, meditation and prayer, a beautiful sunset, a child's laughter, a slow meal with friends—anything that calls our attention to the sacredness brimming in each moment and reminds us that we have a role to play in creating a better future, right here and now, is our friend. New wine is all around us, friends. May we keep ourselves open and ready to embrace it.

CHAPTER 2

The Parable of the Mustard Seed

STORIES WE CAN TASTE

When I was small, I was fortunate that my family lived in between my maternal grandparents on the left and my maternal great-grandmother on the right. I spent countless childhood days wandering between their houses, creating a treasure trove of memories that still bring me so much joy. It was truly a gift to grow up where I did, when I did, in such close proximity to them.

My great-grandmother was an especially dear person. Her name was Wilma, but we affectionately called her "Maw Bill." She was in her sixties when I was born, and passed the year I turned twelve, but we packed so much joy and meaning into those too few years. Her little kitchen table was one of the most sacred places on the planet. Tables have a way of becoming that, don't they? A table isn't just a piece of furniture, it's a place where stories are shared. Around that table she introduced me to generations of family members that I had never met but somehow felt like I knew. Maw's table became a place where our family past met our family present and began to shape our family's future, all while we were making sandwiches. They may have seemed small, that table and those moments, but their impact is still being felt in my life, all these years later.

Speaking of those sandwiches we'd make at Maw's, there was just something different about them. In some ways, they were like the sandwiches we made at home—some bread, some kind of meat, and maybe a slice of tomato. Pretty run-of-the-mill in terms of ingredients. What made a sandwich at Maw's next-level, the secret ingredient, was the condiment we used: French's mustard in a glass jar.

I know what you're thinking. Yellow mustard is far from some exotic, secret ingredient. You're totally right. Except for one thing—the glass jar made it feel so fancy. When I was a kid the squeeze bottle had recently been introduced, so at my house, when we had sandwiches, you would pick the bottle of mustard up, shake it violently, then twist the nozzle hoping against hope that you'd avoid that initial watery discharge that was less than appetizing. There was just something about the clicking of the knife against the side of the jar that, for me, made a standard yellow mustard rival the ultra-bougie Grey Poupon that I'd seen on television commercials. That experience, tied to my maw, around her table, is probably somehow subconsciously connected to why mustard is still my favorite condiment today. While my preference now is for something like a stone-ground or horseradish mustard, I'm guessing my allegiance is not just one of taste alone but also experience. I realize that mustard can be a controversial topic. If you are a mayonnaise person, I don't judge you. I don't understand it, but I don't judge. There's something about mustard and that pungent, slightly tangy flavor that I absolutely love.

Which brings me to another of Jesus's parables, often called the "parable of the mustard seed." One of my favorite things about Jesus's storytelling is that he told stories that we can taste. From wine to bread to mustard, Jesus's parables are packed with the flavors of everyday life. That should not, however, lull us into thinking that these stories are going to reinforce our expectations and assumptions. Jesus is not simply propping up conventional wisdom. In fact, he's doing the exact opposite. The parable of the mustard seed is a challenge to the way his listeners, then and now, envision the kingdom of God.

ONE PARABLE, THREE VERSIONS

As we saw with Jesus's parable about wine and wineskins, the mustard seed shows up in all three of the Synoptic Gospels, and while similar, there are variations in the stories that will matter as we move to interpretation. Once again, I'll share each Gospel writer's version of the parable, highlighting the differences in each for later discussion. First, moving chronologically, is Mark.

> He also said, "With what can we compare the kingdom of God, or what parable will we use for it? It is like a mustard seed, which, when sown upon the ground, is the smallest of all the seeds on earth, yet when it is sown it grows up and becomes the greatest of all shrubs and puts forth large branches, so that the birds of the air can make nests in its shade."
> (Mark 4:30-32)

Now, notice how Matthew takes the parable from Mark and slightly adjusts it.

> He put before them another parable: "The kingdom of heaven is like a mustard seed that someone took and sowed in his field; it is the smallest of all the seeds, but when it has grown it is the greatest of shrubs and becomes a tree, so that the birds of the air come and make nests in its branches."
> (Matthew 13:31-32)

I would argue some of Matthew's changes are inconsequential for the meaning of the parable. For example, Mark has the mustard seed "sown upon the ground," without reference to who did the sowing, while Matthew adds that "someone" did the sowing. It's not a shock to our systems that a person was involved in planting the seed.

However, there are a couple of interesting shifts from Mark to Matthew that deserve our attention. Notice the location of the sown seed. For Mark it is sown "upon the ground." That doesn't necessarily mean or imply that the place where the seeds were planted was somewhere you'd expect to find a cultivated plant growing. Mustard seeds could grow wild, in both meanings of the word: unplanted by humans and they would also grow uncontrollably, potentially taking over the area in which they took root. In Matthew that location is more specific, the mustard seed is sown "in [a] field." A field is exactly the kind of place where we might expect to find a plant being intentionally cultivated.

Another innovation Matthew makes to Mark's version of the parable is found in just what happens to the mustard seed after it is planted. In Mark it becomes "the greatest of all shrubs." Matthew agrees that it becomes the greatest of all shrubs, at first, but then it further transforms into a tree. Keep these two images in mind—the shrub and the shrub-turned-tree—and let's turn to Luke's account. We will once again find similarity and dissimilarity with what came before.

> He said therefore, "What is the kingdom of God like? And to what should I compare it? It is like a mustard seed that someone took and sowed in the garden; it grew and became a tree, and the birds of the air made nests in its branches."
>
> (Luke 13:18-19)

Luke has the same basic plot: a mustard seed is sown and becomes something much larger than one might expect. However, Luke's details diverge again from those of Mark and Matthew. For Luke, the seed is planted not haphazardly on the ground or intentionally in a field but in a garden. In my experience this seems to be a further movement toward cultivation and control. A field is more managed than just planting a seed somewhere, and a garden is even more managed than a field. Between Mark and Luke, there is a taming of the wildness of the mustard seed.

The other significant difference between Luke and the previous renderings is what the tiny mustard seed becomes in the end. Remember, for Mark it was a great shrub and for Matthew a great shrub-turned-tree. Luke skips the shrub altogether. The mustard seed goes from a small kernel planted to a tree in which the birds nest.

This contrast between location and what is produced matters for how we understand this parable, and I'll come back to it as we move through this chapter. For now, let's keep them in the backs of our minds as we talk about mustard seeds.

SMALL BEGINNINGS

"The kingdom of heaven," Jesus began, "is like a mustard seed." My guess is this isn't what his listeners expected to hear. Whether it was Jesus who called them "the smallest of all the seeds" or if that was, as some scholars believe, an explanatory note from Mark to his audience who were unfamiliar with the plant, it's not quite correct. Orchid seeds, for example, are smaller than mustard seeds. For some, this disqualifies Jesus, dashing his credibility on the rocks of bad botany. I tend to think this is a note from the writer, but either way, I don't need Jesus to be an expert in spermology (the scientific study of seeds). The point is that mustard seeds are very small and likely had taken on a proverbial meaning as a result. We find reference elsewhere in the New Testament to this metaphor linking mustard seeds to smallness, but also the potential that this smallness holds.

The point is that mustard seeds are very small and likely had taken on a proverbial meaning as a result.

In Matthew 17 Jesus had just returned from the Mountain of Transfiguration. He returned from that climactic moment with Peter, James, and John only to find the other disciples in a bit of a pickle. Immediately Jesus was met by a father who had brought his son for an exorcism. The other disciples had attempted to cast out the demonic presence in the boy, but they were unable to get the job done. Jesus was clearly annoyed by their failure, because it reflected their lack of trust.

> Jesus answered, "You faithless and perverse generation, how much longer must I be with you? How much longer must I put up with you? Bring him here to me." And Jesus rebuked the demon, and it came out of him, and the boy was cured from that moment. Then the disciples came to Jesus privately and said, "Why could we not cast it out?" He said to them, "Because of your little faith. For truly I tell you, if you have faith the size of a mustard seed, you will say to this mountain, 'Move from here to there,' and it will move, and nothing will be impossible for you."
>
> (Matthew 17:17-20)

Jesus compares the kind of trust needed to advance the Kingdom movement to that of a mustard seed, small in size but powerful in practice. Luke also includes a reference to mustard-seed-sized faith, but in that context, Jesus was responding to a request from his disciples for increased capacity to trust.

> *The apostles said to the Lord, "Increase our faith!" The Lord replied, "If you had faith the size of a mustard seed, you could say to this mulberry tree, 'Be uprooted and planted in the sea,' and it would obey you."*
>
> (Luke 17:5-6)

Both of these passages refer to the capacity of small amounts of trust to do big things, even moving trees and mountains (at least at the level of metaphor). Taken together we can see how the mustard seed functioned proverbially as an image for smallness and a contrast for growth beyond our expectations. That being the case, Jesus's use of this image in the parable of the mustard seed must, at least in part, intend some of our focus to be on the seeming insignificance of the seed planted, and how the growth of that seed teaches us something about what the kingdom of God is like.

TREES, BRANCHES, AND BIRDS

Next, we focus the result the seeds produce. As we've seen there is a discrepancy between the three Gospels as to what grew from the seed that was planted. Mark says the greatest of shrubs, Matthew agrees until the shrub morphs into a tree, and Luke skips the shrub stage altogether in favor of a tree. What is the issue here? Why don't the three versions of this parable agree? To begin to understand the difference between the parables we have to turn our attention to the tradition in which Jesus was formed.

Over the years I have often heard Christians say something like this: "I am a New Testament Christian. I focus on the red letters, not the stuff in the Old Testament." Here's the problem with this sentiment: Jesus was Jewish; he was formed in the Jewish tradition (a.k.a. the Old Testament / Hebrew Bible); and his life, teaching, and work only make sense within the framework of the Jewish tradition and scriptures. With that in mind, one of the most helpful questions to ask about something Jesus says in the New Testament is, Does this have some sort of grounding within the Hebrew Bible?

The image of a tree, with birds sheltering in its limbs, is one that has several connections within the Hebrew Bible. In Psalm 104, God is being celebrated as the Creator and Sustainer of all things, including caring for animals.

> *Bless the* LORD, *O my soul.*
> *O* LORD *my God, you are very great.*
> *You are clothed with honor and majesty…*
>
> *You make springs gush forth in the valleys;*
> *they flow between the hills,*
> *giving drink to every wild animal;*
> *the wild asses quench their thirst.*
> *By the streams the birds of the air have their habitation;*
> *they sing among the branches.*
>
> *(Psalm 104:1, 10-12)*

The poetic language of the psalmist envisions a God whose care and faithfulness extend to all creation—providing shelter and protection for our avian friends. This reminds me of Jesus's teaching about worry in the Sermon on the Mount, where he reminds his followers, whose concern for daily bread was not a metaphor but a reality, that God cares for and feeds the birds, so they can trust God to do the same for them (Matthew 6:26).

The image of birds resting/nesting in branches in the biblical tradition goes beyond just the idea of protection and provision. It is also associated with power, kingship, and empire. There are three specific examples, two that focus on the leadership of other nations and one that is grounded in messianic expectation. Our first example comes from the writing of the prophet Ezekiel. In chapter 31 the prophet makes a pronouncement against the Egyptian pharaoh, comparing him to a "cedar of Lebanon, with fair branches and forest shade, and of great height, its top among the clouds" (v. 3). The description continues to describe the branches of this powerful cedar:

> So it towered high
>   above all the trees of the field;
> its boughs grew large
>   and its branches long,
>   from abundant water in its shoots.
> All the birds of the air
>   made their nests in its boughs;
> under its branches all the animals of the field
>   gave birth to their young,
> and in its shade
>   all great nations lived.
> (Ezekiel 31:5-6)

To use this metaphor, the tall cedar whose branches provide shelter and shade for the animals, including birds, is a way of describing the power and reach of the Egyptian Empire. Other peoples, nations, looked to Egypt for the stability and security of their world. But not so fast, says the prophet. The tree had grown too big for its britches, to mix metaphors. Pride and ego had infiltrated the heart of the pharaoh and, as a result, the mighty tree would be felled.

> Foreigners from the most terrible of the nations have cut it down and left it. On the mountains and in all the valleys its branches have fallen, and

its boughs lie broken in all the watercourses of the land, and all the peoples
of the earth went away from its shade and left it.

> On its fallen trunk settle
>   all the birds of the air,
> and among its boughs lodge
>   all the wild animals.

(Ezekiel 31:12-13)

The powerful empire, the lofty cedar, can no longer provide shelter or shade, because it has been cut down. The branches on which the birds nested have been broken. Ezekiel 31 is a tale of power gained and power lost, all wrapped up in this image of trees, branches, and birds.

The next reference to this set of images being applied to other nations is found in Daniel 4, and involves a frightening dream experienced by the Babylonian king, Nebuchadnezzar. In his dream the king saw a large, tall tree, the top of which reached into the heavens. It was lush and productive, its fruit providing food for everyone. Then there is a familiar line:

> *The animals of the field found shade under it,*
>   *the birds of the air nested in its branches,*
>   *and from it all living beings were fed.*
>   *(Daniel 4:12b)*

Suddenly, in this dream, a figure identified as a "holy watcher" declares that the tree is to be stripped of its branches and left as nothing but a stump and roots, bound with iron and bronze. None of Nebuchadnezzar's magicians or diviners could offer an interpretation of the dream; they were baffled. But Daniel, also called Belteshazzar, makes his entrance into the story, and he is deeply distressed by the dream, because he knows full well who the trees symbolizes: Nebuchadnezzar, the king whose dream he is interpreting. Because of his pride, Nebuchadnezzar would be temporarily removed from power, until he acknowledged God, and not himself, is sovereign.

The tree that you saw, which grew great and strong so that its top reached to heaven and was visible to the whole earth, whose foliage was beautiful and its fruit abundant, and which provided food for all, under which animals of the field lived and in whose branches the birds of the air had nests—it is you, O king! You have grown great and strong. Your greatness has increased and reaches to heaven, and your sovereignty to the ends of the earth.... You shall be driven away from human society, and your dwelling shall be with the wild animals. You shall be made to eat grass like oxen, you shall be bathed with the dew of heaven, and seven times shall pass over you, until you have learned that the Most High has sovereignty over the kingdom of mortals and gives it to whom he will. As it was commanded to leave the stump and roots of the tree, your kingdom shall be reestablished for you from the time that you learn that Heaven is sovereign.

(Daniel 4:20-22, 25-26)

Both of these examples, Pharaoh in Ezekiel and Nebuchadnezzar in Daniel, are essentially about God judging the nations for amassing power and wealth, and as a result failing to acknowledge God as the source of their abundance. That is not the only use of this metaphor, however. Ezekiel offers another picture of a tree, birds, and branches that is grounded in messianic hope.

In Ezekiel 17, the prophet is offering a vision of hope beyond their current predicament of exile. To summarize the context briefly, the last king of Judah was a man named Zedekiah. He had, according to the prophets Ezekiel and Jeremiah, foolishly rebelled against Babylon. The results were swift and painful. Before Zedekiah's eyes were gouged out, the final thing he saw was his sons being killed. Then he was blinded, put in chains, and taken to Babylon. That was the end of the monarch connected to the family line of David. The problem with this end-of-the-line moment is that God had promised David, in 2 Samuel 7, that one of his descendants would always reign over the throne of Judah. That pledge was not just in jeopardy, it was effectively ended by the Babylonians.

From that context of exile, the prophet Ezekiel offers a message of hope and possibility. The fire might have died down, but the embers remain lit. Ezekiel employs what is now a familiar image for us, that of a "lofty cedar."

Thus says the Lord God:

> *I myself will take a sprig*
> > *from the lofty top of the cedar;*
> > *I will set it out.*
> *I will break off a tender shoot*
> > *from the topmost of its young twigs;*
> *I myself will transplant it*
> > *on a high and lofty mountain.*
> *On the mountain height of Israel*
> > *I will transplant it,*
> *and it will produce boughs and bear fruit*
> > *and become a noble cedar.*
> *Under it every kind of bird will live;*
> > *in the shade of its branches will nest*
> > *winged creatures of every kind.*
> > > (Ezekiel 17:22-23)

In poetic language and imagery, the prophet paints a hopeful picture of a restored Davidic monarchy, which would also mean the restoration of the people in the land. Exile will end, he says, God will transplant power from the empires that have oppressed Judah, and will instead give it to the rightful king, the descendant of David, who will lead the nation to become the powerful, tall tree in whose branches the birds (i.e., the nations) can find shade. This is a hopeful messianic vision in which the power structures of the world flip and Judah comes out on top.

In both uses of the imagery, the proud nations being laid low by God, and the renewal of the Davidic hope and kingdom as a result of that judgment of the nations by God, these trees, branches, and birds function symbolically to talk about power, leadership, and the right to rule the world, also known as empire.

WHAT KIND OF PLANT?

This journey through the references to this image in the Hebrew Bible is central to how I have come to understand the meaning and challenge of Jesus's mustard seed parable. Specifically of interest is how the Gospel writers shift the kind of plant the mustard seed produces, from shrub to shrub-tree to tree.

It's likely the seed/plant intended in this parable is black mustard, which does not grow into a tree like a cedar of Lebanon, but an unseemly shrub that can range in size from eight feet to ten feet tall.

In his *Natural History*, Pliny the Elder says that "mustard which has so pungent a flavour, that it burns like fire, though at the same time it is remarkably wholesome for the body. This last, though it will grow without cultivation, is considerably improved by being transplanted; though, on the other hand, it is extremely difficult to rid the soil of it when once sown there, the seed when it falls germinating immediately."[1]

In some ways a mustard plant is a bit weed-like. Once it takes root, even when cultivated intentionally, it can be hard to manage. Isn't it so fascinating that Jesus would choose this, a small mustard seed that germinates into an uncontrollable shrub, to describe the kingdom of God? Remember, that is what he's doing with this parable in Mark,

31

comparing the kingdom of God vision and movement he has launched to a mustard seed that becomes a shrub. Why would he choose this image? It would have surely been shocking to those listening to him. The kingdom of God could not be small, and it would not be a shrub. Ezekiel said it himself: this kingdom would be a transplanted shoot from a cedar that would grow into a lofty tree. Jesus's compassion to a seed and shrub would have been laughable on the one hand and infuriating on the other. Yet I think it is the core to understanding his idea of God and of God's kingdom.

In some ways a mustard plant is a bit weed-like. Once it takes root, even when cultivated intentionally, it can be hard to manage.

As we saw with the new wine and wineskin, Jesus's position was that God's kingdom—think of it as not just geography but also how justice was maintained within it—could not be experienced in the structures of empire. It could not be empire-lite or empire with a kinder theology. For Jesus, if the Kingdom was to be a radical break with the way things are, with how the world was being run and the resources distributed, then it could not look or operate like empire. So instead of the tall, strong cedar Jesus opts for the unruly mustard plant.

Like mustard, once sown, begins to grow in unwieldy ways, so was Jesus's vision of the Kingdom: spreading person to person, family to family, as people answered the invitation to join a community that was living as if God's future was already a possibility of the present—because for Jesus, it was. He could talk of the presentness, the here and nowness, of the Kingdom because he was enacting and implementing the vision and values of that Kingdom then and there, on earth as it was in heaven. For that announcement, only a mustard plant could do, because it reflected the radical break with the assumptions and expectations that came before. No wonder some heard Jesus's message and found it impossible, impracticable. It wasn't a sudden intervention from God in heaven, but a small seed planted in the ground. The result wasn't going to be immediate; it would take time to germinate and take root. When it did, however, when people began to experience justice—enough food to eat, healing, and liberation—Jesus was convinced that it could not be chopped down like a tree. It would be resilient, more like a weed. Once the birds (imagine those who had been marginalized and excluded by their society) found their place in the shade of this shrub, they would never want to step back out into the searing heat again. To put it another way, once someone had tasted and seen what the world could be, they would never be content with the status quo ever again.

The comparison, then, of the Kingdom to a mustard seed is also a contrast of the Kingdom with the way kingdoms typically work. It's not just about something small becoming something larger, it's also about how that now-larger thing acts and behaves. That is the challenge of the mustard seed parable. It's not just about expansion and development but about how it happens and the values that shape what becomes of it.

At least in Mark. You'll remember that Matthew and Luke both alter the image Mark uses. Mark's version of the parable is, in my estimation, the earliest. Mark wrote around the year 70 CE, a decade or more before Matthew (c. 80s) and as much as forty or fifty years before Luke (c. 110s). This means that Matthew used and edited Mark, and later Luke did the same to both Mark and Matthew. So why would Matthew make the shift from a shrub to a shrub-tree, and why would Luke want to lose the shrub altogether? Let me offer a couple of possibilities.

First, maybe Matthew and Luke were aware of the tradition surrounding the lofty trees with birds among the branches and they were seeking to make it explicit that Jesus was interacting with that tradition.

Building off of that, another possibility is that both writers were a little uncomfortable with the depiction of the Kingdom that Jesus gives in the mustard seed parable. To compare the Kingdom not with strength and power that was evident but with something small, growing out of sight and becoming something unruly could have been too much for them. Might they have wanted to bring the vision of Jesus more in line with the way their hopes were for this movement? This decision is also reflected in the way the ground is described—beginning with something almost wild sounding in Mark (sown upon the ground), to something more cultivated in Matthew (a field), until finally Luke places it in a proper garden. Is it possible that Matthew and Luke, and two thousand years of Christian history, have tried to de-radicalize and domesticate the message and meaning of Jesus? Have we preferred something that felt more proper and manageable to the wildness of his vision?

A MOVEMENT OF
SEEDS AND SHRUBS

One of the challenges of Jesus's parables, which are deeply connected to the context that produced them, is sorting out how we engage and apply them today. What does the parable of the mustard seed mean for us now? What challenges does it offer? What invitations? Those are the questions to which we now turn.

While there are more meanings than space to share them, I will offer four. This parable about the Kingdom is intended to inspire hope among Jesus's followers, then and now. The smallness and insignificance we can feel, both as individual people and communities, aren't the whole story. When we look at the problems and challenges of the world, speaking for myself at least, we can feel almost demoralized. How can I, or even my community, do anything meaningful about the injustice we see all around us? How can we move the needle in any significant way on the climate crisis? What can we do as we witness violence and genocide happening around the world? If we let ourselves, we could just throw up our hands in frustration at the impossible-feeling work in front of us. Yet no matter how small, the good news planted within us is germinating. Even if it's under the surface and unseen, every mustard-seed-sized action taken with love and a dream for a better world bears fruit. Maybe the way we change the world, which is what Jesus seems to be getting at, is to do all the good we can every chance we get, trusting that over time small things can add up to something bigger than the individual parts. In that way this is a story about potential and possibility.

In keeping with the questions above, the mustard seed is also a call to patience. In her poem "Don't Worry," the late poet Mary Oliver writes, "Things take the time they take." Every time I read it, those words are a needed reminder. In a microwave culture, one in which sitcoms have trained us that, in the span of about twenty-two minutes, serious conflict can be introduced and solved, patience can be hard to develop. That's not a criticism of sitcoms, by the way. I love them. It's more an acknowledgment of how important it is to remind ourselves that life, relationships, and pretty much everything that really matters takes time and attention. The buried seed is growing, even if it isn't obvious. Whether it's the state of the world, our own faith journeys, or our relationships, our patience will be a key ingredient. That is especially true internally. Being patient with ourselves, knowing we are in progress and process, is so very important.

The mustard seed parable is also a story about transformation. A seed is buried, but that isn't the end. It continues to grow and change. Somehow, and it just seems almost miraculous to me, that small, planted seed is transformed into something new. There's continuity, but also change. One form is left behind, and a new form is born. In so many ways the story of the mustard seed is the story of our journey toward growth and human flourishing.

In so many ways the story of the mustard seed is the story of our journey toward growth and human flourishing.

Finally, this is a parable that challenges us to hear the radical message of Jesus without attempting to domesticate it or mute its provocativeness. I find it so interesting that many of us who have lived most or all of our lives in the United States have a tendency to import American values into the stories of Jesus. This will become clearer as we move into the latter part of this book, but for now let's just acknowledge that it can be really easy to read a parable, like the one about the mustard seed, and turn it into something that extols the values of capitalism. After all, something small is invested and becomes something much, much larger. That's the American Dream, right? Yet I think in this particular story we find a challenge to the way we've been taught to see the world. We want the lofty cedar tree, don't we? We've been taught and trained to want it. The shrub is unappealing. It doesn't seem powerful, and we've been taught to want displays of strength and power. The shrub isn't impressive to look at, not like the towering cedar with its strong branches. I can empathize with Matthew and Luke here. There is something in us, not just as Americans but as a species, that is pulled toward tall trees and not unruly shrubs. And yet, Jesus has given this to us as his vision of the Kingdom and has invited us to join the movement—a movement of power with, not power over. A movement of justice and compassion, not the status quo and indifference. A movement of mustard seeds and shrubs, not tall trees and strong branches. The challenge I am taking forward personally, as a Christian and a pastor, is to ensure that in my life and work, the mustard shrub never becomes the lofty cedar. Won't you join me?

CHAPTER 3

The Parable
of the Leaven

SOURDOUGH STARTER
AND THE KINGDOM OF GOD

My mother-in-law makes incredible bread. I'm not even what you might call a "bread person." If we go to a restaurant that offers complimentary rolls, I usually pass, which my kids appreciate. But when my mother-in-law bakes bread, I make an exception. Her bread is so fluffy and, for lack of a better term, so bread-y, that I can't pass it up.

Making good bread like that is a process, and one of the key ingredients is to use a "starter." For those of us who are uninitiated (like I was before writing this chapter), a starter is a live, fermented culture comprising flour and water. When those two elements are combined and allowed to ferment, the mixture will cultivate the wild yeast present in the environment. Apparently wild yeast is everywhere, all around us, and when left in a warm spot the visible flour-water mixture interacts with the invisible yeast. Once fermentation begins, the mixture will begin to bubble, and after about a week of feeding it regularly with more flour and water, a starter is born.

The name implies the function. A starter is a leavening agent. When a small amount of this fermented mixture is added to dough, it makes the dough rise. It's what gives my mother-in-law's bread both the airiness and that distinct beer-like flavor. This process reminds me that most of the things we enjoy are a combination and collaboration between humans and the natural world around us. We take things from the earth, combine them, and wait for nature to interact with them to create something nourishing and delicious.

Jesus described the kingdom of God similarly. As we've already seen, Jesus gravitated toward images for the Kingdom that were natural processes (new wine fermenting and a mustard seed growing) and yet, at the same time, required human participation and cultivation. Our next parable is no different. For Jesus, the kitchen could reveal the nature of God's kingdom in powerful ways. We now turn to Jesus's parable about leaven and dough.

ONE PARABLE, TWO VERSIONS

Up until now each parable we have examined is found in all three of the Synoptic Gospels. The parable of the leaven, however, is only included in two of the canonical Gospels, Matthew and Luke. Further, both the parables of the new wine/wineskins and the mustard seed had some interesting and even significant differences from source to source. In the case of the parable of the leaven, that isn't true. Besides a slight shift in the introductory words, the parables are quite consistent with one another.

He told them another parable: "The kingdom of heaven is like yeast that a woman took and mixed in with three measures of flour until all of it was leavened."

(Matthew 13:33)

And again he said, "To what should I compare the kingdom of God? It is like yeast that a woman took and mixed in with three measures of flour until all of it was leavened."

(Luke 13:20-21)

Besides the initial phrasing, the only disunity in these versions is Matthew's use of "kingdom of heaven," which is, as we saw in the introduction, a reflection of respect for the name of God that was and is common within the Jewish tradition. In both Gospels the parable of the leaven follows the mustard seed, which leads scholars to think that perhaps traditionally these two parables were linked, functioning as dual, surprising images for Jesus's vision of God's kingdom. Just as Jesus's comparison of the Kingdom to a shrub instead of a tree would have shocked his listeners, so would the likening of the kingdom to some leaven that a woman hid in some dough.

THE KINGDOM IS LIKE THE KITCHEN

In the mustard seed parable, the action is outdoors—on the ground, in a field, or a garden, respectively—and generated by the masculine sower of the seed (at least in Matthew and Luke; Mark leaves the one who sows ambiguous). Here, in this parable, Jesus shifts the scene to the kitchen and to the activity of a woman baking bread. This was no doubt a counterintuitive image for many of those who heard Jesus's teaching.

First, when describing the Kingdom, we don't expect the monotony and humdrum-ness of daily life. For the teenager in my house, it would be akin to comparing the kingdom of God to his average school day. Almost every day I pick him up in the car rider line and my first question is always, "How was your day?" By now, we both answer in unison, "Boring." Isn't the Kingdom extraordinary? Isn't it something beyond the everyday experiences of chores and homework? Maybe Jesus chooses such a setting for this parable to drive home the point that, in his vision, the Kingdom was present and possible in just these average, ordinary, everyday kind of moments.

Second, Jesus centers the action of a woman in this story. He compares the Kingdom to a woman who hid some leaven in some dough. In a patriarchal society, we might be a little surprised to find a woman as a central character in a story about the kingdom of God. I'm almost certain Jesus's audience would have perked up at this detail. Let's pause to note that, within the Jewish tradition, there were many significant stories that had women at their center: Ruth, Esther, Hannah in 1 Samuel, and Deborah in Judges, just to name a few. And those are just the canonical stories. We find more strong women who play significant roles in the intertestamental literature. This is all true. A woman being included and centered in a story isn't an anomaly for the biblical literature. There are plenty of examples of women who break out of the confining roles society had prepared for them, and, at the same time, that society (like all of them in the ancient world) was still patriarchal.

From that vantage point, men were understood to be strong. They would go to war, hunt, and held pretty much all significant societal leadership roles. Essentially, men faced outward. Women were held, thanks to thinkers like Aristotle, to be weaker, less than their male counterparts. Their job was to take care of the home—birth and raise children, prepare food, and tend to all things domestic. Women faced inward. How unexpected might it be, then, for Jesus to use the image of a woman doing domestic work, baking bread, as a metaphor for God's kingdom? Would this comparison jostle his listeners awake, or perhaps elicit a gasp or two in response?

How unexpected might it be, then, for Jesus to use the image of a woman doing domestic work, baking bread, as a metaphor for God's kingdom?

The parable of the leaven isn't the only place in which Jesus does this, either. Four of Jesus's stories in the canonical Gospels center on the activity of women. The three additional stories include two from Luke and one from Matthew. In chapter 15 of Luke Jesus tells a trilogy of parables about a lost sheep, a lost coin, and a lost son. The parable of the lost coin focuses on a woman who had ten coins but lost one. She turned her house upside down to find it, and when she did, she called her friends and neighbors together to celebrate her lost-but-now-found coin.

Three chapters later, in Luke 18, Jesus tells another story, this one focused on a widow who persistently kept demanding justice from an unjust judge. Her incessant requests were eventually granted by the judge.

The final example comes from Matthew 25, in a parable about ten bridesmaids, five of whom were wise and five who were foolish. The five who were wise took extra oil with them, while the five who were foolish did not. When the bridegroom arrived at midnight, the foolish bridesmaids were unprepared. I'll say more about this kind of parable in the chapters to come, but for now it stands as an example of women being centered in Jesus's storytelling.

This parable isn't just a woman being centered, however. This parable takes it up several notches by comparing this woman and her bread-making activity to the very meaning of God's kingdom. Jesus is challenging his listeners, then and now, to expand our imaginations and press beyond what we think is possible.

A LITTLE BIT OF LEAVEN

What is it about this context (a kitchen) and this medium (leaven and dough) that express Jesus's understanding and vision of the kingdom of God? On the surface, we could point to the fact that a little bit of yeast was able to thoroughly leaven a large quantity of dough. Something small having a significant impact is a standard reading of this parable, but as we saw with the mustard seed, this is only part of the story.

To begin, the use of yeast/leaven in this story in a seemingly positive sense is curious. The word used to describe what is added to the dough in this parable is *zume*, which is translated often as yeast or leaven but describes the fermented "starter" we discussed earlier. When combined with the preposition *en* (in, by, with) you get our word *enzymes*, which are proteins that catalyze the chemical reactions in the human body. Leaven makes things happen.

If you go to a standard Greek lexicon and look up *zume*, you will usually see two definitions. The first is "fermented dough," as we might expect. The second is more metaphorical. Yeast/leaven is something that negatively permeates our attitudes and behaviors. This raises the question, Why does leavening have a negative connotation? The answer is found in how leaven is talked about in the rest of the Bible. In Scripture, even elsewhere in the teaching of Jesus, something being leavened is not a good thing. A few examples might be helpful.

In Exodus 12 the first Passover is instituted. Another name for this is the Festival of Unleavened Bread. The instructions for the seven-day remembrance of the Hebrews' liberation from enslavement in Egypt includes the following command

> "This day shall be a day of remembrance for you. You shall celebrate it as a festival to the LORD; throughout your generations you shall observe it as a perpetual ordinance. Seven days you shall eat unleavened bread; on the first day you shall remove leaven from your houses, for whoever eats leavened bread from the first day until the seventh day shall be cut off from Israel."
>
> (Exodus 12:14-15)

The reason for the command to make unleavened bread is given later in Exodus 12 as is practical: the people needed to leave Egypt and did not have time to wait for the bread to leaven. The removal of the rising agent reflected the urgency of the moment. Reenacting that each year is a way of remaining connected to and grounded in that story. Notice that leaven itself isn't the problem any other time than Passover, but that purging of leaven during that season becomes a metaphor for removing something that could corrupt.

This symbolic use occurs in both Jesus's and Paul's teaching. In passages from Mark 8 and Luke 12, Jesus warns his disciples to be on guard against the influence of different groups that were challenging his movement.

> Now the disciples had forgotten to bring any bread, and they had only one loaf with them in the boat. And he cautioned them, saying, "Watch out—beware of the yeast of the Pharisees and the yeast of Herod."
>
> (Mark 8:14-15)

> Meanwhile, when the crowd had gathered by the thousands, so that they trampled on one another, he began to speak first to his disciples, "Beware of the yeast of the Pharisees, that is, their hypocrisy."
>
> (Luke 12:1)

In both examples Jesus uses the symbol of yeast/leaven in a negative sense to warn his followers to keep specific values and attitudes from creeping into their hearts. In the broader context of the Mark 8 passage, it seems that could focus on the way the community shared their food, leading to enough for everyone. The yeast/leaven here might be symbolic of a stinginess and scarcity approach to food and possessions. This attitude would be deeply detrimental in a community like Jesus's that focused on sharing resources. For Luke, the yeast/leaven is hypocrisy. Either of these attitudes could, like leaven, go undetected in the dough until it was too late. A communal catastrophe could result.

Two final examples can be found in Paul's authentic letters. In Galatians, one of the earliest authentic letters from Paul that we have, we find him on the defensive. After Paul left the Galatian communities, other missionaries came in with a different message, one that began to impact the way the Galatians thought. Paul wrote this letter to defend his message and to call the Galatians to stick with the message he taught them. We can't be totally sure what the opposition message was to the Galatians, because we have only Paul's side of the argument. But he makes it clear that, from his perspective, it would only take a little bit of that thinking creeping in before the community would be overtaken by it.

> You were running well; who prevented you from obeying the truth? Such persuasion does not come from the one who calls you. A little yeast leavens the whole batch of dough.
>
> (Galatians 5:7-9)

Finally, in 1 Corinthians 5 Paul is responding to reports that things at Corinth are going off the rails. To address the problem, Paul uses the metaphor of Passover to call the community to a different way of being.

Your boasting is not a good thing. Do you not know that a little yeast leavens all of the dough? Clean out the old yeast so that you may be a new batch of dough, as you really are unleavened. For our paschal lamb, Christ, has been sacrificed. Therefore, let us celebrate the festival, not with the old yeast, the yeast of malice and evil, but with the unleavened bread of sincerity and truth.

(1 Corinthians 5:6-8)

These few examples point to yeast/leaven being a negative metaphor for attitudes and behaviors that sneak in and corrupt the good dough. Why, then, would Jesus compare the kingdom of God to leaven? How can that image possibly reflect Jesus's understanding or vision?

A WHOLE LOT OF DOUGH

Before we attempt a response to those questions, we have to talk about the ridiculous amount of dough the woman in this story makes. Jesus says the woman in this parable took leaven and mixed it in "three measures of flour." At first glance "three measures" might not seem all that significant. That is, until we translate that amount into the system of the first century. A measure, or *saton* in Greek and *seah* in Hebrew, are the equivalent today of a little over a bushel, or roughly sixty pounds. That is an absurd amount of dough for this woman to be baking and would have produced enough bread to feed more than a hundred people. Such an exaggerated amount leads me to wonder, why would Jesus use such a number or offer such a detail? Is it the equivalent of saying a "bajillion" for us?

In part, yes, I do think this is meant to be seen as a ridiculous exaggeration. But it isn't just that. The specific mention of "three measures" has connections within the Hebrew Bible that will further illuminate what Jesus is saying in this parable. There are three specific instances of this exact amount being referred to. I'll share each before commenting on the possible meaning. The first is found in Genesis 18. God appeared to Abraham in the form of "three men," just prior to the story of Sodom and Gomorrah. Abraham invites the men to stay and be refreshed before continuing on their journey. One of the refreshments that Abraham offered the visitors was fresh-baked bread.

> *And Abraham hastened into the tent to Sarah and said, "Make ready quickly three measures of choice flour, knead it, and make cakes."*
>
> *(Genesis 18:6)*

The second occurrence is found in Judges 6. Gideon was beating wheat in the winepress in an attempt to hide it from the Midianites, Israel's oppressors in that day. He, like Abraham, has an encounter with God in which God calls him to be a liberator for the people of Israel. During that conversation Gideon, also like Abraham, provides hospitality for his divine visitor.

> *So Gideon went into his house and prepared a kid and unleavened cakes from an ephah of flour; the meat he put in a basket, and the broth he put in a pot and brought them to him under the oak and presented them. The angel of God said to him, "Take the meat and the unleavened cakes and put them on this rock and pour out the broth." And he did so. Then the angel of the* LORD *reached out the tip of the staff that was in his hand and touched the meat and the unleavened cakes, and fire sprang up from the rock and consumed the meat and the unleavened cakes, and the angel of the* LORD *vanished from his sight.*
>
> *(Judges 6:19-21)*

Two quick explanatory notes. First, while I am sure many of us know this, a "kid" here refers to a young goat. We can breathe a sigh of relief on that one. Second, the amount of flour given here is an "ephah," which is equal to, you guessed it, three measures.

The final relevant passage comes from 1 Samuel. Here, Hannah, who has given birth to a son thanks to divine help, took him to live and serve at the Tabernacle at Shiloh. She had committed her child, if God would help her conceive, to this service. She took a few items with her to present along with her son: "When she had weaned him, she took him up with her, along with a three-year-old bull, an ephah of flour, and a skin of wine. She brought him to the house of the Lord at Shiloh, and the child was young" (1 Samuel 1:24).

What do these three texts that reference "three measures" have in common? They all involved an encounter of God. Another way of putting it is that in each of these stories—a theophany (visible manifestation of God) for both Abraham and Gideon and going to the Tabernacle for Hannah—the three measures of flour signal the presence of God. Somehow that exaggerated amount of flour became connected with an experience of divine nearness.

HIDING THE LEAVEN

Jesus's parable has an additional surprise for us. We've already seen the Kingdom compared to a woman engaged in domestic work and the staggering amount of dough she leavens. It's also how she goes about doing it. Once again, here's the text from Matthew:

> He told them another parable: "The kingdom of heaven is like yeast that a woman took and mixed in with three measures of flour until all of it was leavened."
>
> (Matthew 13:33)

She took the yeast and "mixed" it in with three measures of flour. Or did she? This is a great example of how the decisions made by translators can sometimes obscure the layers, details, and meaning of a story. The text in Greek does not say the woman "mixed" the yeast with the flour. It literally reads she "hid" the yeast in the flour. The word here is *enkrypto*, which is where we get the word/idea "encryption." The woman "encrypts" the yeast in the flour.

The yeast being hidden, as opposed to the expected "mixed," speaks to Jesus's approach to advancing God's kingdom. It's a process. It takes time. The yeast doesn't instantly overwhelm the dough. What the bakers reading this will know is that to get that really good flavor and rise out of the dough, it will require "proofing." While it seems like the dough is resting, during proofing the fermentation process continues. Even if it is unseen, the yeast continues to break down the sugars and starches present in the dough, which releases carbon dioxide, causing the dough to expand and rise. What a brilliant image for the way Jesus understood God's kingdom!

Jesus chose to build that movement by engaging people and calling them to follow and embrace the kind of values and actions that create a just and generous community.

For Jesus, the Kingdom would not overwhelm in an instant. It also would not be a top-down new order that would be imposed or enforced on anyone. The Kingdom was a way of living, a way of seeing life and our responsibility to care for one another. Jesus chose to build that movement by engaging people and calling them to follow and embrace the kind of values and actions that create a just and generous community.

Take, for example, Jesus's call of tax collectors like Levi and Zacchaeus, or other wealthy people like the rich ruler. He wasn't just trying to expand his donor base. He called people who had been enriched at the expense of their neighbors and who had taken advantage of and perpetuated the system of inequality that defines empire to stop their harmful actions and to share their abundance with their community. That is how the Kingdom advanced, through the transformation of the hearts and minds of people. As they reoriented their relationships to their stuff, they also experienced a healing in their relationship to their community.

One other example of this slow, intentional "proofing" in Jesus's approach to the Kingdom might be helpful. Think about the way Jesus regularly transgressed and transcended the boundaries and barriers that kept some people at a distance. His understanding of the Kingdom was that it could best be seen in the way those who are marginalized and excluded were brought close into community. Be it diagnosis or reputation, Jesus moved toward those who had been othered, and in doing so reflected the compassionate healing nature that marked the presence of God's dream for the world.

The dough needs time to rise, and Jesus understood that any movement that longs to transform the world into a place of justice, peace, and wholeness will also take time. Obedience can be demanded. Compliance can be forced. Transformation and love cannot. Those values that make the world a better place cannot be coerced or imposed. They must be cultivated, and that often happens in the unseen, person-to-person moments for which Jesus was known.

PUTTING THE PARABLE TOGETHER

Up to this point we have looked at the parable in parts or stages. We've explored the metaphors, discovered their connection to the Hebrew Scriptures, and raised several questions along the way. Now we will turn our energies toward pulling all these strands together to discover the message of this parable and what it might mean for us today.

The parable of the leaven is both surprising and subversive. Jesus begins by throwing his listeners off balance by having a woman engaged in the everyday, ordinary tasks of domestic life as the one driving the action of this story. This, for Jesus, was not just a rhetorical device but also a paradigm for the movement. Jesus's Kingdom movement put these kinds of surprising metaphors into concrete, lived community experience.

This parable reflects Jesus's insistence that the Kingdom could be discovered in the everyday ordinariness of life. Planting mustard seeds, storing wine, and baking bread were not tasks of a special realm or qualification. They were not confined to sacred days or experiences. It was the stuff of everyday life that became a window into God's dream for the world.

Jesus's use of leaven as a symbol for the Kingdom and how it advances is especially counterintuitive. While not associated with sinfulness, because of its connection to Passover and the Exodus narrative, leaven had become a metaphor for something that corrupts. Something small could contaminate something much larger. Yet here Jesus flips that metaphor on its head, insisting that the opposite was also true. Some small amount of goodness, justice, hope, and love could permeate and transform in massive ways. The reclaiming of this metaphor reminds us that Jesus regularly did this kind of pushing back on stereotypes and assumptions. No one listening to him probably imagined a "good Samaritan" either.

The use of leaven also likely described well how that kingdom vision of Jesus was received and experienced by the empire and those who benefited from the Roman oppression of Judea. God's kingdom was a corrupting influence, disrupting the social and economic power structures Rome had established. Whether Jesus's movement was a welcome act of liberation and healing or a threat that presented a challenge would all depend on where one sat.

The connection between the "three measures" and the other uses of this exaggeration in the Hebrew Scriptures further call our attention to Jesus's understanding that God wasn't somewhere else, and God's kingdom wasn't somewhen else for someone else. In other words, in contrast to other expectations of his day, Jesus understood that while we are often waiting for God to act or intervene in some way, God is in reality waiting for us to join in and participate in creating a better world. For Jesus, God was experienced as a present reality, not a future intervention. The Kingdom could be experienced in the here and now if we join God in making, or perhaps decrypting, this good news. This is precisely how Matthew, just after he records the parable of the leaven, has Jesus describe his work as a parable-teller.

> Jesus told the crowds all these things in parables; without a parable he told them nothing. This was to fulfill what had been spoken through the prophet:
>
> "I will open my mouth to speak in parables;
> I will proclaim what has been hidden since the foundation."
> (Matthew 13:34-35)

Jesus, through parables like this one, was attempting to make the unseen, under-the-radar, kingdom visible. By inviting people to find both God and the Kingdom in the everydayness of life, Jesus opened for his followers a dimension of reality, a new kind of humanity, that had always been available, if they had eyes to see, ears to hear, and hearts that were open to that possibility.

BAKING FRESH BREAD TODAY

By now it's probably obvious that this ancient parable still has much to say to us today. You have probably already started connecting the dots, but I'll offer a few of my own observations in case they are helpful.

First, God's kingdom is still chock-full of surprises. The moment we assume we have it all figured out, that mystery has been conquered, and all questions answered, the Kingdom says to us, "Not so fast!" In unexpected moments, unlikely places, and through surprising sources, God's kingdom still offers a challenge to our assumptions. A woman hiding some leaven in some dough, a mustard seed growing, and just about any and every moment of our lives can be avenues through which God shows and expands the kingdom of goodness, justice, and peace.

God is looking for partners and collaborators to bring about a better world.

Another meaning, connected to the first, is that God is looking for partners and collaborators to bring about a better world. The grapes must be pressed, the mustard seed needs to be planted, and the dough won't knead itself. God works through cooperation with us, through our creativity, generosity, and effort. We are not background characters in this story; far from it. We are main characters, which means what we do and don't do really matters. Our compassion can move things forward, and our indifference can perpetuate the harm and injustices we see all around us. The entire story of Jesus is one big invitation to join in on the work of making a better future for all of God's kids. I know that can feel daunting, even overwhelming. In the world around us we see violence and genocide, economic disparity and inequality, the worsening climate crisis that puts our collective future in jeopardy, and those are just a few of our problems. It can be hard to know where to start or if little ole me can even make an impact that registers in any meaningful way. Does that sound familiar to anyone else?

In those moments when I'm engulfed in the enormity of the challenges we face and the smallness of what I can do, I try to remember that part of the point of a story like this one is to remind us that small things can have outsized impact. If we each leaven the dough that is right in front of us, and keep doing it as we have the opportunity, then together we can bring about significant change that is greater than the individual parts. Our main job is to keep showing up, to keep alert and engaged. That's exactly what Paul encouraged the Galatian churches to do.

So let us not grow weary in doing what is right, for we will reap at harvest time, if we do not give up. So then, whenever we have an opportunity, let us work for the good of all and especially for those of the family of faith.
(Galatians 6:9-10)

To use the language and metaphor of Jesus's parable here, let's keep showing up to the kitchen. Let's keep mixing the water and flour together, hiding the leaven in, and kneading the dough. Not every loaf we attempt to bake will be perfect. Sometimes they might not rise like we'd hoped they would. Anyone who's spent any time in the kitchen, or anywhere else for that matter, knows that not every batch, project, or goal always turns out like we'd hoped. But we need to stay engaged, keep showing up, and keep our conviction front and center that the way things are right now aren't the way they have to be forever. Remember, a starter is made is by combining the water and flour and leaving it out for the natural yeasts that are all around us all the time to begin to do their work. That, I think, is a powerful metaphor for the way the Spirit moves, unseen, through our acts of love, compassion, generosity, and peacemaking. Our job is to mix up the ingredients we have available and entrust that our efforts will be energized by the Spirit. The point has always been God with us, not God instead of us.

Patience is a key ingredient in baking, creating, and changing the world. Admittedly, that is not my strong suit. Anybody else? I struggle with waiting. When we plant seeds in our garden I want immediate growth, not long days of watering and pulling weeds, or plants that don't produce like I'd hoped. Yet that decision to be present daily in the muck, mire, and frustration is what ultimately produces a harvest. For Jesus, that is how the Kingdom works. It takes time and often expands in ways that cannot be readily seen on the surface. I trust that is happening in my life and yours, and in all the ways we make ourselves present and available to this important work of leaving the world better than we found it. Let's keep our hands in the dough, baking fresh bread, and spreading the goodness of God's dream for the world.

CHAPTER 4

The Wicked Tenants

A SHIFT IN FOCUS

Up until now, with the first three parables we've examined, the focus of Jesus's stories has been short, comparison-driven sayings that image God's kingdom as a kind of process: new wine fermenting and expanding a fresh wineskin, a mustard seed that becomes an unruly shrub, and a bit of leaven that causes dough to rise. The next three parables will mark a shift from short, memorable sayings or images to narrative-based stories with characters, action, and consequences. When we think of Jesus's parables, it's likely these kinds of stories have captured our memories and imaginations most.

Before we turn to the first of these narrative parables, I want to invite us to first acknowledge, and then attempt to bracket, the assumptions and expectations we often bring to the Bible, especially Jesus's stories. Because we are so familiar with the basic narrative arc of these parables, we tend to read them with the built-in assumption that we already know who the characters are supposed to represent: the powerful man/king/landowner is God, a "son" figure is always Jesus, those being punished are always sinners or unbelievers, and so on. These assumptions are formed through years of sermons, Sunday school classes, and Bible studies, but also reinforced by our cultural lenses. We all have lenses through which we read and interpret the Bible; that isn't something we can help. We just have them. Where we live, when we live, our upbringings, life experiences, and both what and how we were taught—all of these shape how we approach everything, including the Bible. It is impossible for a person to not be shaped by the simple fact that we exist in a particular world. While we don't choose the lenses we inherit, our responsibility is to become aware of them and how they influence our interpretations. That awareness allows us to notice how we might be importing and imposing our particular contexts onto and into the texts and stories of the Bible. Remember, Jesus's parables are often about surprise, reversal of expectations, and a challenge to the status quo. That was true then, in his day, and it holds true even now, in ours. If that all feels like theory at the moment, that's okay. In this first parable we will see and engage the importance of our lenses, practically.

GRANDMA MILLIE'S GRAPEVINE

One of my favorite things to do at my maw's house was to go exploring around her property. Toward the back of her land there was an old house that had collapsed in on itself over the years that had once belonged to my great-great-grandma Millie. When Millie comes up, even to this day, someone will always mention that she smoked a corncob pipe. It was and is her signature.

While I wasn't supposed to go poking around in the ruins of her house, I was allowed to play near the small, old cinder block building that was adjacent to what was her home. I loved going back there because there was a Concord grape vine that had grown up the side of the building. How did it get there? Was it planted? Was it wild? No one can remember. We just know that it was there when my grandpa, who was born in the late 1930s, was a kid. It produced the best, juiciest grapes I've ever tasted, and even though I haven't had them in more than thirty years, they remain the litmus test by which all other grapes are judged.

Grapevines and vineyards in the first-century world of Jesus were significant and symbolic, and could be a societal flash point.

When I read Jesus's parables that involve vineyards, like the one we will study in this chapter, my memory takes me back to that little cinder block building in the 1980s, with me feasting on grapes from the family vine. As we will see in this story, grapevines and vineyards in the first-century world of Jesus were significant and symbolic, and could be a societal flash point.

ONE STORY,
THREE TELLINGS

The parable we are talking about in this chapter is often titled "the parable of the wicked tenants." I will want to revisit that title again at the end of the chapter. This story is found in all three of the Synoptic Gospels, but each telling has some unique features that are grounded in how each writer shapes them according to their needs. For the sake of space, I will share Mark's version, the earliest and the source Matthew and Luke used as a template. The parable is found in Mark 12:1-12; Matthew 21:33-46; and Luke 20:9-19.

Then he began to speak to them in parables. "A man planted a vineyard, put a fence around it, dug a pit for the winepress, and built a watchtower; then he leased it to tenants and went away. When the season came, he sent a slave to the tenants to collect from them his share of the produce of the vineyard. But they seized him and beat him and sent him away empty-handed. And again he sent another slave to them; this one they beat over the head and insulted. Then he sent another, and that one they killed. And so it was with many others; some they beat, and others they killed. He had still one other, a beloved son. Finally he sent him to them, saying, 'They will respect my son.' But those tenants said to one another, 'This is the heir; come, let us kill him, and the inheritance will be ours.' So they seized him, killed him, and threw him out of the vineyard. What then will the owner of the vineyard do? He will come and destroy the tenants and give the vineyard to others. Have you not read this scripture:

> *'The stone that the builders rejected*
> *has become the cornerstone;*
> *this was the Lord's doing,*
> *and it is amazing in our eyes'?"*

When they realized that he had told this parable against them, they wanted to arrest him, but they feared the crowd. So they left him and went away.

(Mark 12:1-12)

The standard interpretation of this story goes something like this: the parable (at least in Mark and Matthew) begins with an allusion to Isaiah 5, in which the prophet allegorizes Israel as God's vineyard. This direct reference tells us that the vineyard in this story represents Israel. God is the landowner who had entrusted the land to the tenants, Israel's leaders. God then sent the servants, the prophets, to warn and call the leaders of Israel to a just way of living, but their call was not heeded. The prophets were again and again mistreated and even killed. Finally, God sent the beloved son, Jesus, who was also rejected and executed. As a result of the rejection of the son, God would enact judgment on Israel, which happened in the Jewish-Roman war of 66–73 CE. That judgment culminated with the destruction of Jerusalem and the temple in the year 70 CE. The vineyard was then entrusted to others, that is, the Gentiles, who came to believe in Jesus. That is a reading shared by many scholars and interpreters of this text. They call it a parable about "salvation history." The more I read this parable and sit with the details, however, the more problems I have with some of the assumptions and connections that interpretation makes in the parable. Is there another, valid way to interpret this parable? I think there is. Let's begin at the beginning.

ISAIAH'S SONG OF THE VINEYARD

The parable does begin with what seems to be an allusion to Isaiah 5, a song about a vineyard that was planted by God, but that did not meet the expectations God had for it.

> I will sing for my beloved
> my love song concerning his vineyard:
> My beloved had a vineyard
> on a very fertile hill.
> He dug it and cleared it of stones
> and planted it with choice vines;
> he built a watchtower in the midst of it
> and hewed out a wine vat in it.
> (Isaiah 5:1-2b)

In Mark and Matthew this parable is drawing on Isaiah's poetry for the image of a vineyard being constructed. That being the case, let's continue to read the text beyond the opening lines about the building of the vineyard, because it will be helpful to compare and contrast this passage with what Jesus does in the parable.

> He expected it to yield grapes,
>> but it yielded rotten grapes.
> And now, inhabitants of Jerusalem
>> and people of Judah,
> judge between me
>> and my vineyard.
> What more was there to do for my vineyard
>> that I have not done in it?
> When I expected it to yield grapes,
>> why did it yield rotten grapes?
> And now I will tell you
>> what I will do to my vineyard.
> I will remove its hedge,
>> and it shall be devoured;
> I will break down its wall,
>> and it shall be trampled down.
> I will make it a wasteland;
>> it shall not be pruned or hoed,
>> and it shall be overgrown with briers and thorns;
> I will also command the clouds
>> that they rain no rain upon it.
> For the vineyard of the LORD of hosts
>> is the house of Israel,
> and the people of Judah
>> are his cherished garden;
> he expected justice
>> but saw bloodshed;
> righteousness
>> but heard a cry!

(Isaiah 5:2c-7)

There are similarities between the Isaiah passage and Jesus's parable—specifically the creation of the vineyard and the judgment/removal of the vineyard. Those two events are present in Jesus's parable. However, notice the key difference. The problem in the Isaiah text is not the tenants who are caring for the vineyard. The issue is the vineyard itself. The owner, God, prepared the vineyard to produce grapes, but the result was rotten grapes. The rotten fruit, which we learn from the passage is a reference to the lack of justice in the lands of Israel and Judah, is the cause of the vineyard's removal. In context, Isaiah 5, written likely around the year 740 BCE, is a reference to the impending exiles that Israel and Judah would face in 722 and 587 BCE, respectively. The failure to uphold justice, according to the prophets, would lead to a cataclysmic future for Israel and Judah.

In Mark's version of the story, the issue is not that the vineyard itself will be removed and left vacant, but instead it is that those who had been entrusted with the care of the vineyard will be relieved of their duties and the vineyard would be entrusted to others. That becomes more explicit in Matthew's account of this story: "Therefore I tell you, the kingdom of God will be taken away from you and given to a people that produces its fruits" (Matthew 21:43).

I think this slight difference brings into focus something important: the land itself wasn't the issue. It was how that land, and the resources of it, were being stewarded that was creating the problem. Land was not only practical, a source of both sustenance and shelter, it was also theological. To understand what Jesus is doing in this parable we must also talk about what land meant in the first-century Jewish experience.

GOD'S GREEN EARTH

In the Hebrew Bible the land was not owned by Israel, but by God, and loaned to Israel under the expectation that it would be cultivated, cared for, and justly distributed. What would happen, then, if God's green earth was not being justly distributed? What if someone, for example, found themselves in a mountain of unpayable debt and needed to either sell their land to pay, or lost it as collateral for, a loan?

The Torah, the first five books of the Hebrew Scriptures, which contain the Law, pays special attention to the preservation of justice, specifically providing a societal reset to guard against the gap between the rich and the poor expanding. First, every seventh year was to be a "sabbath year." The ground was given a year of rest. It was not to be plowed, planted, or pruned. Whatever the land produced could be eaten, but it could not be grown as the result of human action. Then, second, after every seven sabbath years, or forty-nine years, there was to be a celebration in the fiftieth year called Jubilee.

> *"And you shall hallow the fiftieth year, and you shall proclaim liberty throughout the land to all its inhabitants. It shall be a Jubilee for you: you shall return, every one of you, to your property and every one of you to your family."*
>
> *(Leviticus 25:10)*

> *"In this year of Jubilee you shall return, every one of you, to your property."*
> *(Leviticus 25:13)*

> *"The land shall not be sold in perpetuity, for the land is mine; with me you are but aliens and tenants."*
>
> *(Leviticus 25:23)*

What happens, then, when people lose their land and Jubilee doesn't come?

The key here is that the land was a gift and a loan from God, and as such could not be perpetually sold, taken, or transferred. To do so would mean families losing their ability to provide for themselves through growing crops and creating products to use in bartering for other necessities. What happens, then, when people lose their land and Jubilee doesn't come?

The prophets warned against this kind of activity, the gobbling up of land by the wealthy few at the expense of the many poor. In the passage from Isaiah 5, after the song of the vineyard, the prophet called out this exact practice:

> Woe to those who join house to house,
>   who add field to field,
> until there is room for no one,
>   and you are left to live alone
>   in the midst of the land!
> The LORD of hosts has sworn in my hearing:
> Surely many houses shall be desolate,
>   large and beautiful houses, without inhabitant.
> (Isaiah 5:8-9)

Those of us raised in a capitalist culture might not see the problem with this activity. After all, it sounds like good business sense, right? Getting more land, expanding operations, building bigger houses—it's practically an American success story. But it isn't a success story. Instead, it's a story about harming and displacing one's neighbors for personal benefit and selling out your community for one's own advancement, luxury, and comfort. What does this practice have to do with Jesus's parable? In a word, everything.

AN ECONOMY THAT WORKED . . . FOR SOME

In the twenties and thirties of first century CE Galilee, where Jesus lived and worked his entire life before he took that fateful trip to Jerusalem, the economy was booming under the leadership of Antipas. He enacted policies of globalization and commercialization that led to a prosperous economy for some people, though the wealth was not shared across social classes. The estimate is that 90 percent of the population in Galilee lived at a subsistence level or worse. The two driving issues they would have faced daily were, How do we eat today? and How do we pay our debts? Knowing this gives a whole new depth to the petitions in the Lord's Prayer, "Give us today our daily bread. And forgive us our debts, as we also have forgiven our debtors" (Matthew 6:11-12). Those aren't abstract spiritual metaphors, but the pressing realities of everyday life for the overwhelming majority of first-century Galilean families.

Imagine this scenario: A family experiences a bad crop, leaving them in a financial hole. They need to plant crops again but can't afford the seed. A wealthy person comes along and agrees to give them a loan that will enable them to plant their fields. This is not just a loan of goodwill or an act of benevolence, though. It comes with strings. The interest rates, in blatant violation of the commands of the Torah (see Leviticus 25:35-37), could be as high as 60 to 200 percent for crop loans. In order to get the loan, the land they lived on, worked on, and depended on for their existence and sustenance would be taken as collateral. If the harvest could not cover the debt and the family could not pay off the loan, the land was confiscated, and they were displaced. The options on the other side of displacement were to work a trade or become tenant farmers, possibly on the very land that they once called their own. Can you imagine how these displaced families felt? With all this context in mind, let's return to Jesus's parable and ask how his first-century listeners might hear this parable differently than we have.

WHOSE VINEYARD IS IT?

In Jesus's narrative parables our impulse is to assign meaning to characters so that we can better understand the story. That is a necessary task. How we do that and to whom we assign the identity of the characters is central because it will shape our interpretation. That raises a very important question: Who is this vineyard owner?

The parable begins, as we've seen, with the construction and planting of a vineyard. The implication is that this isn't an established vineyard that has been around and passed down for generations. This is a new vineyard. Land is being converted, commercialized. That is our first clue to the identity of this vineyard owner.

The term used to describe the one doing the converting of land to vineyard varies between the Gospels. In Mark it is simply a "man" (Greek: *anthropos*), and in Luke it is slightly different, a "[certain] man" (Greek: *anthropos tis*). It is Matthew who gives a further identifier for this person by referring to him as "he," but then adding that he was a "landowner" (Greek: *oikodespótēs*). This word is a compound word, comprising the words for house (*oîkos*) and master (*despótēs*). The "landowner" isn't just someone who owns a piece of land or property. They would represent the antagonists in the scenario described above, those who were adding "house to house and field to field," further deepening the economic disparity between the rich-and-getting-richer and the poor-and-getting-poorer. It's an interesting detail Matthew adds, and it leads me to a question: Would Jesus use as an image or representative for God a character who represents the opposite of God's justice? Could it be that the landowner who constructs the vineyard isn't the God character? What if the vineyard owner is not the benevolent God loaning land to Israel, but a wealthy, predatory landowner taking advantage of his neighbor to expand his portfolio? Let's move forward with the parable assuming that this is the case. How will that change or shape our interpretation?

THE TENANT'S SITUATION

Most treatments of this parable haven't paid much attention to the tenants, beyond the fact that they are the "bad guys" in the story. Even though this is a parable, a created story, Jesus's audience would have known this experience in their bones. For them, these tenants were three-dimensional characters who were responding to real circumstances. What motivated them? Why did they respond to the vineyard owner this way? What did they hope to achieve?

For just a moment, imagine yourself in their shoes. You had land that had been passed down in your family for generations, and you had worked that land, cultivated it by adding your own blood, sweat, and tears as your parents and grandparents did before you. What is the reward for all that work? Your family land was taken through legal, but unjust, means and now you must come back to the land of your ancestors as a tenant under someone else's direction. How would that feel? Can you empathize with the feelings of anger, resentment, betrayal, and embarrassment that real people in this situation would have felt?

Can you empathize with the feelings of anger, resentment, betrayal, and embarrassment that real people in this situation would have felt?

A new vineyard would not produce economically for five years. This detail alone gives us insight into the wealth of the landowner who constructed the vineyard. He could wait for the vineyard to become profitable, all the while fronting the overhead for the construction costs and paying the tenants to care for the property. A vineyard was a financial risk. What if, when the fifth season arrived, the grapes did not produce as expected? A person of modest means could not afford to launch such an endeavor. Day after day these tenants went to work cultivating a vineyard whose fruit they would only marginally benefit from, while their labor further enriched those who had taken advantage of the fragile economic state of their families. Is it possible that some of the people who heard Jesus's story would feel some identification with and sympathy for the tenants in this story?

The response of the tenants to the slaves (retainers, those who were the go-between and did the dirty work between the elites and the common people) who came to collect the landowner's share of the produce was violent. The purpose of the tenants' action will depend on the perspective from which it is seen. From the viewpoint of the landowner, they are trying to steal his land and are violating his property rights. The tenants, however, who understand this land to belong to God and as entrusted to them as an inheritance, would likely frame their actions as a reclamation of that which was taken from them unjustly. Another perspective to consider is that of the vineyard itself. If we allow the vineyard to become a character in the story we might ask, Who does the vineyard recognize or know? The absentee landlord who views the land as a means to an end? Or the hands of the vinedressers who cultivate and harvest the abundance it produces?

When the landowner sends his son, who would stand to inherit this land, he is not met with the honor and respect that the owner expected. He is instead killed and cast out because, the tenants reason, if the heir is removed, maybe they could regain their property rights.

Whether or not that was a logical assumption would soon be tested. The landowner himself would come and hold the tenants to account and then give the care of the vineyard over to others. In Mark, Jesus asks and answers the question:

> *"What then will the owner of the vineyard do? He will come and destroy the tenants and give the vineyard to others."*
>
> (Mark 12:9)

> *"What then will the owner of the vineyard do to them? He will come and destroy those tenants and give the vineyard to others."*
>
> (Luke 20:15b-16)

In Matthew Jesus asks the question, "Now when the owner of the vineyard comes, what will he do to those tenants?" but he does not supply the answer. Instead, his listeners respond, "They said to him, 'He will put those wretches to a miserable death and lease the vineyard to other tenants who will give him the produce at the harvest time'" (Matthew 21:40-41).

Either way, the result is the same: the landowner holds the tenants accountable by doing unto them as they had done unto his servants and son. While we have been conditioned to accept that this is the God figure in the story I have to ask, Is this really what God is like? Is Jesus telling a story that ends with divine violence as the solution to human violence? To complete our interpretation of this parable let's take a further step and place it within its Gospel context.

HOLY WEEK CONTROVERSY

Remember that when Jesus told this story, his intended audience immediately understood the implication of the parable; they didn't need to ask for clarification or explanation.

> *When they realized that he had told this parable against them, they*
> *wanted to arrest him, but they feared the crowd. So they left him and*
> *went away.*
>
> (Mark 12:12)

Their response tells us two things about Jesus: he was becoming a problem for them, and the crowds loved him. But who is the them here? To find the answer we need to go back one chapter, to Mark 11, which also marks the beginning of what Christians call Holy Week. During this week Jesus brought his kingdom of God movement to Jerusalem and was ultimately executed by the empire. Let me walk us, briefly, through the events that led up to Jesus telling this particular parable.

Following Mark's account, the week began with Palm Sunday and what is called the Triumphal Entry of Jesus and his followers into Jerusalem around the time of Passover. This was more of a faux triumphal entry, however, a lampoon of the ways Roman leaders and armies would flex their muscles. A Roman governor, like Pilate, would enter a city like Jerusalem at Passover with a show of force, riding on war horses, flanked by soldiers decked out in armor and armed to the teeth. Jesus entered on a donkey, accompanied by his followers who fanned branches and celebrated as if God's kingdom had finally come.

The following day, Monday, Mark sandwiches Jesus's temple action between a story about the cursing and subsequent withering of a fig tree. Two important points about this. First, this was not a "temple cleansing." It was a prophetic demonstration, a warning about what the fate of the temple institution would be if its stewards did not change their ways. Second, the fig tree is often used as a symbol of Israel, and here it seems to be about the temple institution specifically. The events of Holy Monday are related to, and are symbolic judgments upon, the Jerusalem temple. We should not assume that the temple itself, meaning the stones and structure of the building, was the problem for Jesus. This is not Jesus verses Judaism or Jesus verses the temple, as it has so often, and I might add inaccurately and dangerously, been described throughout Christian history. Jesus's action was directed at those who were in charge: the temple authorities.

Rome, the empire that dominated and ruled Judea in the first century, administrated their territories through local collaborators. When they conquered a territory, they would entrust a person from among that group of people to collaborate with them to manage the populace. There were a few qualifications for the role. The person would have been wealthy, they would have to have exhibited loyalty to Rome, they had to have been able to ensure the payment of the tribute owed to Rome, and they would have maintained Roman law and order in the territory. Originally, this role was given to the family of Herod the Great. After his death in 4 BCE his territory was divided between three of his sons, with Archelaus gaining control of the area that included Jerusalem and the temple. However, in 6 CE Rome removed Archelaus from that position, opting instead for direct rule through Roman governors, like Pilate, who governed from 26–36 CE. This didn't solve all their problems, because they still needed local collaborators to keep things operating smoothly among a population that resisted and rejected Roman boots on what they understood to be God's soil. This is where the temple aristocracy came into the picture. Rome chose to make the temple—that is, the leadership— the center of collaboration. This means that the temple authorities— a small, wealthy, and powerful group—were actually benefiting from the oppression of the rest of the people. Jesus was not in opposition to Jews or Judaism; he was Jewish! Instead, Jesus's focus was on the injustice being perpetrated by the wealthy and powerful few, who were using the sacred space as a smokescreen and protection for their crimes.

A similar situation existed in Jeremiah's day, which is why Jesus quoted from Jeremiah during his temple demonstration when he called the temple "a den of robbers." His opposition was not to the temple as sacred space but to the transformation of the sacred space into a cover for the profane actions of a few.

When Jesus entered the temple during Holy Week and publicly demonstrated against the injustices to which it gave shelter, the priestly aristocracy picked up right away that this was about them. By Holy Tuesday they'd already had enough. Who does this Jesus guy think he is? they wondered. Where does he get the authority to challenge us?

Again, they came to Jerusalem. As he was walking in the temple, the chief priests, the scribes, and the elders came to him and said, "By what authority are you doing these things? Who gave you this authority to do them?" (Mark 11:27-28).

Their assumption is that only God would have the authority to pronounce judgment on the temple and its leaders. For Jesus to do such a thing he would need to show his credentials to speak on behalf of the Divine. What on his résumé gave him the standing to do and say these things? In classic Jesus fashion, he responded to their question about his authority with what might seem like an unrelated question about John the Baptist.

> *Jesus said to them, "I will ask you one question; answer me, and I will tell you by what authority I do these things. Did the baptism of John come from heaven, or was it of human origin? Answer me." They argued with one another, "What should we say? If we say, 'From heaven,' he will say, 'Why then did you not believe him?' But shall we say, 'Of human origin'?"—they were afraid of the crowd, for all regarded John as truly a prophet. So they answered Jesus, "We do not know." And Jesus said to them, "Neither will I tell you by what authority I am doing these things."*
> *(Mark 11:29-33)*

This question about John isn't as out of place as it seems. John's movement was also grounded in a critique of the temple authorities. The message of John, calling people to repent and to be baptized for the forgiveness of sins, was an act of subversion. The temple, for John, had become corrupt and unable to fulfill its true function. As a result, his baptism movement was offering an alternative to the temple institution. For the leaders to affirm John's movement would mean that (1) they were agreeing with John's indictment, that their leadership was corrupt; and (2) it would raise a question about why they didn't listen to his call for change. John and Jesus had similar issues with the authorities, and both led movements of resistance and challenge, albeit with differences as we saw in chapter 1. John replaced the temple with water, and Jesus chose a table.

Our parable in this chapter immediately follows this exchange about authority. The tendency to see the temple authorities as the tenants in the parable and Jesus as the rejected and murdered son is one way to interpret this passage, but I want to offer another interpretation. In reality, the authorities had more in common with the landowner. We know historically that it was not uncommon for high-priestly families to own large estates like the one depicted in this parable. Imagine, for example, if one of the temple leaders owned a large vineyard in Galilee. He would not be present on-site, because he lived in the south, in Jerusalem, thus the need for tenants to care for the land and crop. Does that sound familiar? It is the very context Jesus creates in this parable.

THE CHALLENGE
OF THE PARABLE

The temple authorities knew Jesus was telling this parable to critique them, but the question we must ask if we bracket the traditional interpretation of the parable for a moment is, How did this parable work as a critique of the authorities? My proposal is that the story itself is the critique, not specific characters in the story. Using a familiar scenario, one in which the authorities themselves had participated and benefited, Jesus offers a warning. If you don't amend your ways and act justly, eventually people will reach the limit of what they can take and will lash out in violence. Eventually the tensions would spill over into a peasant revolt against their aristocratic oppressors. The landowner in the story does not respond by saying, "Wow! I've really learned my lesson!" Instead, they crush the rebellion, and the system keeps right on rolling and benefiting those at the top.

Without change, without justice being done on earth as it is in heaven, destruction would await, and the very institution they expected to be their salvation would be torn down stone by stone.

The combination of Roman rule and temple collaboration boiled over in 66 CE, as regional anti-taxation protests and religious tensions reached a fever pitch. Rome, in the year 70 CE, razed both Jerusalem and the temple in response. Through this parable Jesus is warning the temple establishment that the luxury and benefit they currently enjoyed at the expense of their neighbors would not last. Without change, without justice being done on earth as it is in heaven, destruction would await, and the very institution they expected to be their salvation would be torn down stone by stone. My hunch is that Jesus would have preferred to have been wrong about this one. Is this a parable about "wicked tenants"? Perhaps. Is it a parable about unjust landowners?

Absolutely. Is it a parable that warns about the consequences of the unbridled enrichment of the few at the expense of the many? You can take that to the bank.

THE MORE DIFFICULT PATH

It may seem like a parable so rooted in a particular first-century context might not have much to say to us almost two thousand years later, but that isn't the case. There are several important applications and questions that emerge from the reading I have offered.

First, we have to talk about God, specifically the images we use for God and the assumptions we make about what God is like. If we believe God is violent and vindictive, we can easily justify our own violence and vengeance. If we understand God's approach to those who oppose God's dream for the world (think enemies) to be about elimination and not transformation, we could lose the entire plot and excuse ourselves from Jesus's call toward enemy love. If we think of God as an absentee landlord, that can translate into a theology that locates God elsewhere—sure maybe God pops in to bibbidi-bobbidi-boo something occasionally, but God's primary residence is somewhere else. Instead, God is right here, with us, among us, in us. That is how Jesus understood God, as a present experiential reality that cares about the birds, flowers, and us.

A second important application is perhaps most uncomfortable because we have to talk about money. The economic implication of this parable tells us what we already know, even if we don't want to recognize or see it: societies with a large and growing gap between the rich and the poor are less healthy, less stable, and less safe. According to the Federal Reserve, the top 0.1 percent of American households own almost 14 percent of the wealth. The top 1 percent control more than 30 percent of the resources. The bottom 50 percent of American households possess 2.5 percent of the country's wealth.[1] And the gap is widening. I am convicted and convinced that part of following Jesus means taking his teaching about money seriously. It means working to ensure that the inequalities and injustices that our economic system is fraught with do not go unnoticed or unchecked. While most of us don't have the power or influence to just change the way things work, we do have our voices and our votes. We also can work to ensure that the way we think about and use our resources matches our convictions about how the world should be. We must understand that in Jesus's day the idea of politics, economics, and religion being separate was unheard of. It is a myth we have told ourselves to insulate us from the cogitative dissonance that arises when we hear the words of Jesus but find them too difficult. Where our treasure is, so goes our hearts. What we value we protect. The call of Jesus and evidence of the arrival of God's kingdom are good news proclaimed to and for the poor. How different would everything be if the church, collectively, embraced the invitation and challenge to join Jesus in that work of doing justice and loving mercy?

Finally, this parable offers a critique and warning about the spiral of violence. The story opens with economic violence, which is met with retaliatory physical violence, but it doesn't stop there, does it? When one person punches another, the fight doesn't end after the original puncher gets their nose bloodied. The landowner doesn't take the actions of the tenants as a lesson to end his predatory practices; he ramps up the conflict with retaliatory violence on the tenants. The truth about violence is that it never brings real, lasting peace and it is never simple or measured. Like a game of ping-pong, the brutality goes back and forth with ever-increasing acceleration. No one escapes unscathed from the physical, mental, and emotional damage that redemptive violence brings with it.

Jesus lived in a world, like ours, that presented choices. He could have taken the path of violent resistance to the empire and its collaborators. Others did and not long after his lifetime. He also could have taken the option of withdrawal. Instead of engaging he could have formed a little enclave of disciples who resonated with his teaching and spent his time away from the very contexts that led to his death. But Jesus didn't do that either. The story of his temptations in Matthew 4 indicates to us that he might have wrestled with which path to take, but ultimately, based on his convictions about how the Kingdom would come and what its values were, he chose to engage nonviolently. If our species has a long, meaningful future ahead of us, we must learn to take this more difficult path. It is not easy, but it is what makes for peace, justice, and a transformed world.

THE CORNERSTONE
OF A NEW WORLD

Jesus ends this parable with a reference to Psalm 118. He quotes verses 22 and 23, which say, "The stone that the builders rejected has become the chief cornerstone. This is the Lord's doing; it is marvelous in our eyes." It is often assumed he is talking about himself, that he will be rejected by the powers that be but vindicated by God in resurrection. Part of that is not just about his physical life but also the message for which he lived and died. The kingdom of God vision might be rejected by many, but its vision of justice and peace are the foundation for a new world. This is the world of which God dreams and for which we must work.

CHAPTER 5

The Wedding Party

WHAT HAVE I GOTTEN MYSELF INTO?

One spring morning a couple years back I walked onto our front porch with a cup of coffee, my computer, and a Bible ready to start my day. It was an absolutely gorgeous morning. My neighbors had just mowed their lawn, so the scent of fresh-cut grass filled the air, both a delight and an assault on my allergies at the same time. I settled into a chair to begin my task for the day, which just so happened to be preparing the sermon for the coming Sunday. I was in a crowdsourced series, the focus of which was passages of scripture that people in my community had struggled to understand. On this particular morning, I looked at the list and the text for the week was a parable found in both Matthew and Luke, but not in Mark, that is often titled "the parable of the wedding feast" or "the parable of the great banquet." I turned to Matthew's version of the story and immediately let out a groan. "What have I gotten myself into?" I wondered.

If this parable, especially Matthew's version, is new for you, you'll see what I mean in just a moment. This cursory front porch reading wasn't my first pass through this parable, but this sermon would be the first time I'd ever tackled talking about what it meant. I had instant buyer's remorse, but I had committed to working through the texts submitted by community. As the old saying goes, I was stuck between a rock and a hard place—or so it seemed. What emerged from my study of this parable was a surprise, a new-to-me lens that would shape how I read all of Jesus's stories. That lens has already been on display throughout this book, but I have my experience of wrestling with this parable, which I have come to refer to as "the parable of the wedding party," to thank.

FRATERNAL TWIN STORIES

So far, the parables that we've examined have been really similar across the different versions. Even though a word might be different here or there, the overall story, and the context in which it was told, have been in sync across Mark, Matthew, and Luke. The parable of the wedding party changes that. While the two versions have similarities, there are also significant differences in both content and context. They are related, but obviously not identical, like fraternal twins. This is something we know very well at our house, because my oldest daughters are fraternal twins. Even though people sometimes get them confused for each other, they are very clearly not identical. In fact, the younger of the two shares more of a resemblance with her younger brother than with her twin. At the same time, they still possess that "twin magic," the closeness and connection that often mark the relationship between these siblings.

The two versions of this parable have a similar relationship. It's evident that the same general story is beneath the two versions, a story about a feast and invited guests who refuse to attend, but there are also several differences. Let's look at both passages, starting with Matthew.

Once more Jesus spoke to them in parables, saying: "The kingdom of heaven may be compared to a king who gave a wedding banquet for his son. He sent his slaves to call those who had been invited to the wedding banquet, but they would not come. Again he sent other slaves, saying, 'Tell those who have been invited: Look, I have prepared my dinner, my oxen and my fat calves have been slaughtered, and everything is ready; come to the wedding banquet.' But they made light of it and went away, one to his farm, another to his business, while the rest seized his slaves, mistreated them, and killed them. The king was enraged. He sent his troops, destroyed those murderers, and burned their city. Then he said to his slaves, 'The wedding is ready, but those invited were not worthy. Go therefore into the main streets, and invite everyone you find to the wedding banquet.' Those slaves went out into the streets and gathered all whom they found, both good and bad, so the wedding hall was filled with guests.

"But when the king came in to see the guests, he noticed a man there who was not wearing a wedding robe, and he said to him, 'Friend, how did you get in here without a wedding robe?' And he was speechless. Then the king said to the attendants, 'Bind him hand and foot, and throw him into the outer darkness, where there will be weeping and gnashing of teeth.' For many are called, but few are chosen."

(Matthew 22:1-14)

You can see why this story gave me pause. The standard interpretation of stories like this is to locate God as the powerful figure, like a king, and in this story the king is violent and seemingly unreasonable. Being thrown into outer darkness is a bit much for a wardrobe malfunction. Luke takes a dramatically different, softer approach.

Then Jesus said to him, "Someone gave a great dinner and invited many. At the time for the dinner he sent his slave to say to those who had been invited, 'Come, for everything is ready now.' But they all alike began to make excuses. The first said to him, 'I have bought a piece of land, and I must go out and see it; please accept my regrets.' Another said, 'I have bought five yoke of oxen, and I am going to try them out; please accept my regrets.' Another said, 'I have just been married, and therefore I cannot come.' So the slave returned and reported this to his master. Then the owner of the house became angry and said to his slave, 'Go out at once into the streets and lanes of the town and bring in the poor, the crippled, the blind, and the lame.' And the slave said, 'Sir, what you ordered has been done, and there is still room.' Then the master said to the slave, 'Go out into the roads and lanes, and compel people to come in, so that my house may be filled. For I tell you, none of those who were invited will taste my dinner.'"

(Luke 14:16-24)

The punishment in Luke's version fits the crime. There's no weeping or gnashing of teeth in outer darkness, just the withdrawal of the invitation to those who refused to come in the first place. That is a significant change, and it isn't the only one. There are several key differences as each author adapts (what was likely) the original story.

First, the contexts in which each of the stories occurs are dissimilar and reflect how Matthew and Luke want to use the parable. In Matthew the parable of the wedding party comes immediately after the parable of the tenants, which we looked at in the last chapter. To refresh our memory, that story is told during Holy Week and during a controversy surrounding from where Jesus's authority came to do and say things that were pronouncing judgments upon the temple. The parable of the wedding party is then followed by a question about paying taxes to Rome. To understand Matthew's meaning, that context is critical to keep in mind.

Luke's version of the parable comes earlier in the story, several chapters before Jesus enters Jerusalem to begin Holy Week. Instead, the story is told while Jesus was at a Sabbath meal hosted by one of the leaders of the Pharisees. Before the parable of the great banquet, Jesus first offered a parable about humility, hospitality, and the added benefit of avoiding social embarrassment.

> When he noticed how the guests chose the places of honor, he told them a parable. "When you are invited by someone to a wedding banquet, do not sit down at the place of honor, in case someone more distinguished than you has been invited by your host, and the host who invited both of you may come and say to you, 'Give this person your place,' and then in disgrace you would start to take the lowest place. But when you are invited, go and sit down at the lowest place, so that when your host comes, he may say to you, 'Friend, move up higher'; then you will be honored in the presence of all who sit at the table with you. For all who exalt themselves will be humbled, and those who humble themselves will be exalted."

> He said also to the one who had invited him, "When you give a luncheon or a dinner, do not invite your friends or your brothers and sisters or your relatives or rich neighbors, in case they may invite you in return, and you would be repaid. But when you give a banquet, invite the poor, the crippled, the lame, and the blind. And you will be blessed because they cannot repay you, for you will be repaid at the resurrection of the righteous."
>
> *(Luke 14:7-14)*

After that teaching another guest at the meal offered what I assume he thought was an appropriate, impressive response. It was the catalyst, however, for Luke's version of the wedding party parable. As a general rule, if Jesus responds to something you say or do with a parable, you are probably in trouble.

> One of the dinner guests, on hearing this, said to him, "Blessed is anyone who will eat bread in the kingdom of God!" Then Jesus said to him, "Someone gave a great dinner and invited many."
>
> *(Luke 14:15-16)*

As with Matthew, the context in which the parable occurs affects its meaning. The placement of the parable is not the only difference between the versions. There are details that are unique to each story. In Matthew it is a wedding party being thrown by a king for his son. Luke's telling is more ambiguous. The feast is given by "someone." Also in Luke, the setting is not a wedding but a "great dinner." Here's a fun fact: the Greek word for "great" is *mega*. It's a "*mega* dinner" with a large guest list.

Further differences include the violence that occurs in the version in Matthew and the absence of violence in Luke. That will also factor into the interpretation of each story. Finally, while both stories make use of the rule of three (a storytelling convention that groups details in three to help listeners understand), they each apply it differently. For Matthew it is found in the triple invitation to the wedding party—first to the invited guests, then a second attempt to invite that same group, and finally to everyone else. In Luke the rule of three appears as the originally invited guests make excuses for their absence at the great banquet—the purchase of land, the purchase of oxen, and a new marriage, respectively.

Now that we have set each story in its narrative context in the Gospels and noted several of the key differences between each version, we can turn our attention to teasing out the meaning of each story.

HOSPITALITY AND THE KINGDOM OF GOD

Up until now we've primarily focused on one version of each parable, noting the significant differences if there were any. In the case of the parable of the wedding party / the great banquet, the two are so divergent that taking that approach would obscure the meaning of each. Matthew's take on the parable is more challenging to interpret and will get most of our time in this chapter. So before we attempt to unravel that more complex narrative, let's look at what Luke might be doing with the parable in his Gospel.

On one level we could understand Luke's edition of the parable to be about hospitality and social embarrassment. The circumstances of a meal and Jesus's teaching on not taking the most prominent seat or only inviting social equals to a feast are central to the parable. If someone threw a feast and only invited those who were of equal status, the potential for embarrassment if those guests could or would not attend would be high. In the honor/shame culture of Jesus's world, losing face in a situation like this was no small thing. The shame and potential loss of social capital as a result could taint the host's reputation moving forward. These honor/shame dynamics are also at play in Matthew's account as well. The way to avoid such embarrassment is to invite people whom the host knows will turn up for a feast, those who would be excluded and unable to reciprocate the host's generosity. The result would be satisfied guests who would no doubt celebrate the host's kindness by saying all the good things about them to others. Not only does the host avoid shame but they also increase their honor.

That meaning can be found in the story, but there is something else, something deeper, happening as well. Jesus tells the story in response to another guest saying, "Blessed is anyone who will eat bread in the kingdom of God!" (v. 15). There are two details here that catch our attention. First, this parable, like the others, is about the kingdom of God. Specifically, it connects the idea of the Kingdom to a feast, which, as we've already seen, is a common image associated with it. Second, remember that Jesus's understanding of the Kingdom is not a future reality that will, at some point, be imposed on the world by God. Instead, it can be a present experience if we change our minds and hearts and join God in making it visible by living justly and compassionately. That's why food was such a central part of Jesus's ministry. Meals are about the sharing of life's most basic necessity, and one that, then and now, has been used as a tool of discrimination and exclusion. What is eaten and with whom it is eaten were not just utilitarian acts of chance but intentional statements about connection, community, and belonging. For Jesus to blur the lines and transgress the boundaries of who was invited to his meals was enacting the kingdom of God practically and in real time.

If those who eat in the Kingdom are blessed, then why not invite them to dinner now? The very act of doing so brings the Kingdom into the present.

If the dawn of the Kingdom would mean the end of hunger and injustice, Jesus's call here isn't just about protecting honor—it's about making the kingdom of God, and the practical, transformative justice that marks its arrival, a present experiential reality. If those who eat in the Kingdom are blessed, then why not invite them to dinner now? The very act of doing so brings the Kingdom into the present.

SPEND THE MONEY ON THE PARTY

Any time I give advice about marriage or parenting, I usually call it descriptive and not prescriptive. I am by no means an expert in either.

I gladly share my experience but would never imagine that it would be universally helpful. When preparing for a wedding, I do offer couples a piece of prescriptive advice that I believe to my core. After two-plus decades of presiding over "I dos" I can say, without hesitation, that the best decision a couple can make is to spend the bulk of their money on the party that follows the ceremony. A wedding ceremony is usually short, and couples often report that it's all a little bit of a blur. The party after the ceremony is where the memories are made and the celebration happens.

It sounds like the king in Matthew's story did just that—he prepared a wedding feast to celebrate his son's marriage. Except, similarly to Luke's version of the parable, no one on the guest list actually came to the feast when it was ready. Imagine all those tables, each one with a place setting and escort card, empty. As we saw previously, this would be a massive social embarrassment, and not just to any ol' rich person. This act of social indifference was directed toward the king and his son! In an attempt to preserve his reputation, another call was extended for the invited guests to come to the party. This time the invitation was made even more irresistible, as the king described the decadent food that would be on the menu. Yet those on the guest list still refused to attend the celebration. Some of them went so far as to mistreat and kill the king's representatives. What more could the king do? He prepared the feast, invited the guests, and rang the dinner bell. His generous invitation was snubbed not once, but twice, and the second time the ungrateful guests even killed the messengers. To reclaim some dignity, the king had no choice but to exact revenge on the guests-turned-murderers by sending the military to kill them and destroy their city.

As the invitation was expanded to any and all, the king must have felt a little vindicated as he looked out over the wedding venue teeming with energy and excitement. There was one person among the crowd who stuck out like a sore thumb, however. One guest in particular was not dressed appropriately for the occasion. The king's response was swift and forceful—there would be no more embarrassment surrounding this party. The improperly dressed man was bound and thrown out of the party and into the "outer darkness," a place of weeping and gnashing of teeth, and the polar opposite of a celebration.

Before we submerge ourselves in the details of this parable to see what we might discover, let's begin by acknowledging (and hopefully bracketing) the standard interpretation we've probably heard. In that interpretation the king and son are an obvious allusion to God and Jesus. The wedding party is the great, future messianic banquet. The king's representatives are the prophets and missionaries who extended the invitation to join God's kingdom, and those who refused to attend are those in Israel who refused the summons to the feast. As a result, they were punished by God (through Rome in 70 CE), and their place at the celebration was offered to the Gentiles instead. The final scene, with the improperly dressed guest, is usually interpreted as a reference to righteousness or proper faith in Jesus. Anyone can join this party, but they must, in this view, be properly dressed.

A PROBLEMATIC READING

This perspective can be found in most commentaries on Matthew's Gospel, but it is fraught with issues. First, as we saw in the previous chapter, just because there is a powerful figure with a son in the story does not mean we must jump to the conclusion that they are stand-ins for God or Jesus. More than just the role being played, we must ask about the personality, about how the figure shows up in the story. For many of us, the idea of God using violence is bound up in the very character of God. The question this raises is an important one.

Does God need to resort to violence to get the job done? Throughout both halves of the Bible, and the traditions that birthed them, this question has been answered differently. Some writers and practitioners have concluded that God, from time to time, might need to respond to humanity with a little smiting. Others have developed a vision of God as nonviolent. The call to beat swords into plowshares is in the Bible (Isaiah 2:4; Micah 4:3), but so is the call to beat plowshares into swords (Joel 3:10). Those texts are in a conversation with one another and us about how we show up in the world. It's more than that, though. The central question is about God's character. If God is violent, then as God's image bearers, we can be too. If God is nonviolent, then our violence is not a divine act but a human failure to fully embrace our role to embody God's image to the rest of creation. In his teaching and practice Jesus aligned with the vision of God as nonviolent. The father awaiting his lost son did not lash out at his child when he came home. He definitely could have. The situation between the king in our parable and the father in Luke 15 isn't all that dissimilar. Both have taken a reputational hit. Both have been embarrassed by the actions of others. Yet the father in Luke 15 ran to embrace his son. He had no time for speeches; he did not need to shame his returning son. No doubt the kid already carried plenty of that with him. Instead, he threw a party, and when the older son refused to join out of bitterness and frustration, the father didn't send an army to destroy him. The father went out to convince him to join the celebration. For Jesus, God keeps a DJ and party planner on retainer, not an army.

Additionally, seeing God as the originator of violence is a decision we make at the expense of Jesus's specific teaching on the issue. In Matthew 11, while speaking on the importance of John the Baptist, Jesus describes the Kingdom as the sufferer, not the source, of violence.

From the days of John the Baptist until now, the kingdom of heaven has suffered violence, and violent people take it by force.

(*Matthew 11:12*)

This is a key distinction that we need to keep in mind: there is a violent response to the Kingdom message, not a Kingdom message advanced with violence. We'll come back to this king figure soon, but for now I want to note that, in my estimation, connecting this character with God is an interpretive mistake.

Jesus was Jewish, his first followers were Jewish, and his message was deeply rooted in and formed by his faith tradition.

A second problem with the conventional reading of this parable is that it feeds into anti-Semitic interpretations of the Jesus story. The idea that Christians (although no one would have used that term or thought of Jesus's teaching or community as a different religion at the time), that is, Gentiles, have replaced the Jewish community is called replacement theology, also known as supersessionism, and it lies at the root of toxic Christian theologies that have unleashed untold violence on our Jewish siblings. Jesus was Jewish, his first followers were Jewish, and his message was deeply rooted in and formed by his faith tradition.

Finally, this reading does not take into account the context in which this story is told in Matthew. Remember, Luke and Matthew locate this story in different places in their narratives, and where/when it appears isn't a random decision. The story is told where and when it is told exactly because of where and when it is told. Let's turn our focus to that larger context and how it shapes our interpretation of this challenging story.

DEATH AND TAXES

We know that the parable of the wedding party takes place during Holy Week and just after the parable of the wicked tenants/unjust landowner. The similarities with that preceding parable are fairly obvious, even with a casual reading. But what comes after this parable? Interestingly, it is Jesus's response to a question about taxes.

> Then the Pharisees went and plotted to entrap him in what he said. So they sent their disciples to him, along with the Herodians, saying, "Teacher, we know that you are sincere, and teach the way of God in accordance with truth, and show deference to no one, for you do not regard people with partiality. Tell us, then, what you think. Is it lawful to pay taxes to Caesar or not?" But Jesus, aware of their malice, said, "Why are you putting me to the test, you hypocrites? Show me the coin used for the tax." And they brought him a denarius. Then he said to them, "Whose head is this and whose title?" They answered, "Caesar's." Then he said to them, "Give therefore to Caesar the things that are Caesar's and to God the things that are God's." When they heard this, they were amazed, and they left him and went away.
>
> (Matthew 22:15-22)

There are a couple important details in this interaction that deserve our attention. First, to quote Admiral Ackbar in *Star Wars: Return of the Jedi*, "It's a trap!" There really is no win for Jesus here. If he responded with a no, that taxes should not be paid to Caesar, then he would be guilty of treason and face a brutal Roman response. Conversely, if he said yes, taxes should be paid to Rome, then he would be seen as a collaborator with Rome against his own people.

This conversation wasn't benign or theoretical. Taxation was one of the flash points for the Jewish revolt against Rome in 66 CE. That wasn't a new tension. Already, in the year 6 CE, there had been a rebellion led by Judas the Galilean against Roman taxation. Paying tribute to Rome, especially while they occupied the land God had entrusted to Israel, was a tension that simmered throughout the decades of the first century and finally boiled over in the revolt against Rome of 66–72 CE. The question of paying taxes to Rome was a clarifying one. Where did Jesus stand on this pivotal issue?

Some commenters like to argue that Jesus does some fancy footwork—or in keeping with the theme from above, a Jedi mind-trick—and stumps his questioners, avoiding giving an answer and foiling their plans. I don't think he's avoiding the question. He answers it, and his answer is what was surprising to the coalition trying to trip him up. He didn't say "Yes, pay taxes," or "No, don't pay taxes." He asked them to show him a coin. Which means...Jesus didn't have a coin on him. His response, "Give therefore to Caesar the things that are Caesar's and to God the things that are God's," isn't saying, "Pay taxes and tithe." The response is a third way between collaboration, on the one hand, and violent rebellion, on the other. Jesus's response is to opt out of the system altogether. You can't pay Caesar's tax if you don't carry Caesar's coin. The problem wasn't just that Rome was taxing the Jewish population while occupying God's land. It was the entire system of empire and the way it had twisted its tentacles around every part of their world, including the economy. We've already seen this at play in the parable of the wicked tenants/unjust landowner. The importing and imposing of Roman values and economics had created a culture of injustice and inequality. Jesus's Kingdom vision was about realizing the justice and enough-ness that are God's dream for the world, and to do that would require a radical break with the values of empire, including the economy. His community was known for sharing resources and eating common meals. When he invited people to join his movement, especially the wealthy (like tax collectors and rich rulers), his first invitation was to divest from their economic interests. Then and now, this kind of response leaves us amazed, stunned, and baffled.

JESUS'S WARDROBE MALFUNCTION

With this context in mind, let's return to the parable of the wedding party. From this lens the king and son characters are not God and Jesus. They are representative of Roman power. The guests who refuse to attend the wedding feast are anti-taxation protestors whose violent response to Rome's governors brought about Rome's counterviolence. They were not met with the wrath of God, but the wrath of Caesar. Matthew's version of this parable takes as a backdrop the Jewish revolt of 66–72 CE, an event in the story's future but the author's past. Read from the location of Jesus's day it is a warning against using violence to accomplish what they believed was God's will. Read from Matthew's day it is an impassioned "I told you so."

But what do we do with the little addendum Matthew adds to the original parable? Who is the improperly dressed guest at the wedding party? There is debate among scholars around the wedding garment. Some say that the garment would be supplied by the host, so to not wear it was an offensive act to the host. Either way, whether brought by the attendee or provided by the host, the interpretation doesn't change. The improperly dressed guest is Jesus himself. His approach to resistance to Rome was not to use violence, but to opt out of their system and to begin living in an alternative community he called the kingdom of God. Of course, this is Holy Week. We know Rome's response will be to "bind him hand and foot, and throw him into the outer darkness, where there will be weeping and gnashing of teeth." We also find in this parable a foreshadowing of Jesus's moment before the authorities. When the king asked the guest where his wedding garment was, he received no response. The guest "was speechless," as was Jesus only a handful of chapters later.

> *Then Pilate said to him, "Do you not hear how many accusations they make against you?" But he gave him no answer, not even to a single charge, so that the governor was greatly amazed.*
>
> (Matthew 27:13-14)

In many ways this parable encapsulates Jesus's message (the kingdom of God) and his method (nonviolent resistance) like none other. It displays his passion for the kingdom of God and its collision with Roman values. Rome knew exactly how to deal with violent revolutionaries. What they couldn't fathom were those who chose nonviolence and sought to live in creative and just ways, even when it cost them everything. Jesus was an enigma to the empire. He still is.

EMBRACING DISCOMFORT

What are some practical takeaways from this parable? There are several. First, we have to talk about our vision of Jesus. As we saw with God in the last chapter, our assumptions about where to locate Jesus and his message within his stories are often shaped by the values that have been instilled in us from the cultures in which we live. We gravitate toward the powerful, when Jesus is found among the powerless. We admire the wealthy, when Jesus is present among the poor. We see characters who do not fulfill the obligations of empire and assume they are the "sinners," when they are really the Christ-figures of the story. The cross can seem extraordinarily foolish from the lens of empire. But for those who are experiencing the transformative impact of the kingdom of God on earth, it is the very power of God.

The cross can seem extraordinarily foolish from the lens of empire. But for those who are experiencing the transformative impact of the kingdom of God on earth, it is the very power of God.

I propose we start looking for Jesus in his stories by first finding those who are suffering, being excluded, or punished. It's not a hard and fast rule, but a helpful guideline that brings our attention to angles we often miss. Jesus is the improperly dressed wedding guest. Jesus is the third servant who buries the talent (opts out). Jesus is not praising a widow for giving all she had to live on to the temple treasury; he's calling out a system that would take it in the first place. And so on.

This interpretation also does the uncomfortable thing by asking us to think about with whom and what we are in collaboration and participation. Stories like these make me uncomfortable because my life is, well, pretty comfortable. What do citizens of the world's largest economic superpower do with these stories? One option is to sanitize and soften them. We make the wedding garment about right beliefs, the buried talent about laziness or unfaithfulness, and the widow's mite an act of generosity to be imitated. That takes the discomfort and challenge away from these stories, and if parables like these are meant to do anything it is to challenge the way we see and disturb our comfort.

Another response is to just ignore the challenge with which Jesus presents us. We could bury our heads in the sand and only focus on our "spiritual lives." The problem with that is that Jesus really never differentiated between the everydayness of life and some special, higher spiritual realm. How we pray is a spiritual action, but so is how we spend our money.

The other option is to embrace the challenge and discomfort of this text and others. We can listen to it, and allow it to interrogate our lives and responses, in hopes that we can experience transformation and join God in making God's dream come true—the work of creating a more just, generous, compassionate, and peaceful world. Here are some questions to get us started:

How does what we buy and where we buy impact those who make the item?

With whom am I collaborating and is that good for me, my neighbor, or the world?

Is my participation in x, y, z helping realize God's dream, or is it perpetuating a human nightmare?

Am I willing to begin changing the way I manage my excess if it would mean the opportunity for others to have enough?

Within the metaphor created by the parable, what are the ill-fitting wedding garments that I need to shed?

There are so many more questions we could ask, but these are a handful to get the conversation started. Embracing the invitation of this parable will surely make us uncomfortable at times. Some people might be annoyed with the questions we ask or the way we adjust our lives because of them. There will be costs associated with living differently in a culture that seems to value more for one over enough for all. On the other hand, there are all the possibilities and hopes of God's dream for the world coming true. Another way of talking about that is human flourishing. That, I am convinced, is God's dream for all of God's kids.

On that spring morning when I sat down with a cup of coffee to read Matthew 22, I had no idea how relevant this parable would be for my own experience. If we allow it to disturb us, and if we take its challenge seriously, it could change our lives, and the world, for the better.

CHAPTER 6

The Workers
in the Vineyard

THE DISAPPOINTMENT
OF THE FIRST PAYCHECK

The year I turned sixteen my life changed in two remarkable ways. First, I gained a newfound freedom when I got my driver's license and a car. I'll never forget the feeling of nervous and excited energy I had pulling out of our driveway for the first time without a parent seated next to me evaluating my driving. The second change was precipitated by the first. Now that I had the freedom to drive, I also picked up the responsibility to find my first job. My first opportunity at gainful employment came at the local CVS. A few days a week and most Saturdays, around thirty hours total, I'd put on the company-issued red smock to stock shelves and work the register, all in anticipation of the payday to come. After all, that very year the minimum hourly wage went from $4.75 to a whopping $5.15. All the fun I missed out on— the movies and games and dates—was totally going to be worth it when that paycheck finally came. Except it was underwhelming to say the least. I don't know what I expected, but the number printed on that cartoonishly large check was not it. I assumed there would be more numbers on it, that's for sure. That first experience with working for a wage was definitely eye-opening and was less of a surprise (but as much of a disappointment) moving forward.

The point isn't evacuating earth for a better life in heaven someday, but transforming earth so that all of God's kids can have a better life today too.

When it comes to Jesus's stories, or any other part of faith or theology, I find most people don't think economically. I didn't for a very long time. Sure, there are some Bible verses pastors use to encourage church members to tithe or the televangelists who use faith to manipulate well-intentioned people out of their resources, but that's not what I am talking about. Once again, we are talking about our lenses, both how we look at Scripture and what we look for in Scripture. When money, say the wages a worker is paid, comes up in a text is that just window dressing in the story or is it an important element— even a character—in the story? I have come to believe the latter. In the territory we have already covered, we've seen how questions of who owned the land (a key component of wealth in an agrarian society) and how they gained access to it, and paying or not paying taxes have both a theological and economic implication. Those are not two opposites occasionally bumping into each other. They are deeply intertwined. In Jesus's world they acknowledged a fact that we have been trained to ignore. Economics are a kind of lived theology. How the world is carved up, how people do or not have access to daily bread, are not just about the economy. They are commentary on and the result of what we ultimately believe about God's dream for the world. The separation of how we spend economically and what we believe theologically have caused us to miss the "on earth" bit of the Lord's Prayer. The point isn't evacuating earth for a better life in heaven someday but transforming earth so that all of God's kids can have a better life today too.

This conversation will be important to keep in mind as we turn our focus to our last parable. Jesus's story about the workers in the vineyard, perhaps more than any of the others we've explored, will ask us to think both theologically and economically. If we accept the challenge, it will unlock meanings that we might have overlooked, not only for this parable, but for the whole of the Bible.

A RECURRING SETTING

The parable of the workers in the vineyard is its own story but shares many similarities with the parable of the wicked tenants. Before we examine those shared connections, let's begin with first hearing the parable. One last note before we go forward. Unlike the other parables we have studied, all of which appeared in at least two of the canonical Gospels, the parable of the workers in the vineyard appears only in chapter 20 of the Gospel of Matthew

> "For the kingdom of heaven is like a landowner who went out early in the morning to hire laborers for his vineyard. After agreeing with the laborers for a denarius for the day, he sent them into his vineyard. When he went out about nine o'clock, he saw others standing idle in the marketplace, and he said to them, 'You also go into the vineyard, and I will pay you whatever is right.' So they went. When he went out again about noon and about three o'clock, he did the same. And about five o'clock he went out

and found others standing around, and he said to them, 'Why are you standing here idle all day?' They said to him, 'Because no one has hired us.' He said to them, 'You also go into the vineyard.' When evening came, the owner of the vineyard said to his manager, 'Call the laborers and give them their pay, beginning with the last and then going to the first.' When those hired about five o'clock came, each of them received a denarius. Now when the first came, they thought they would receive more; but each of them also received a denarius. And when they received it, they grumbled against the landowner, saying, 'These last worked only one hour, and you have made them equal to us who have borne the burden of the day and the scorching heat.' But he replied to one of them, 'Friend, I am doing you no wrong; did you not agree with me for a denarius? Take what belongs to you and go; I choose to give to this last the same as I give to you. Am I not allowed to do what I choose with what belongs to me? Or are you envious because I am generous?' So the last will be first, and the first will be last."

(Matthew 20:1-16)

There are several analogous details between the workers and the tenants. For both stories the action is centered in a vineyard. I would argue that the vineyard is not just a background detail or inconsequential setting for the story, but that, as I mentioned previously, it is itself a kind of character in the story. Additionally, the two stories each focus on a landowner who is looking for workers to assist with caring for his vineyard. While day laborers and tenants are somewhat different roles, they are alike in the fact that people who do not own the land— or perhaps used to and no longer do—are being brought onto the land to work it for someone else's ultimate benefit. Finally, the pair of stories ends with controversy. In the story of the tenants it is the violent usurping of the vineyard and the subsequent punishment. For our story in this chapter, it is about how much the workers were paid for their labor. In the narrative world of the story could we even imagine this to be the same vineyard and same landowner? Either way, it is extremely likely that Jesus's audience, and Matthew's for that matter, would have known real people and had real experiences like those described in Jesus's parable.

MOVING BEYOND ASSUMED READINGS

Like the others we've explored, this parable has a standard reading or interpretation that goes something like this: God is the landowner who recruited workers for his vineyard. These workers were hired at different times of day, meaning some worked more than others. At the end of the day each worker, those who worked the longest and those who worked the least, were compensated with the same amount for their labor. Those who worked the longest were frustrated and complained about getting the same pay for much more work. The interpretive assumption here is that the workers who came first are symbolic of the Jews and the late-arriving workers are Gentiles. God, in God's grace, had offered salvation (symbolized by the denarius paid to each worker) to Jews and Gentiles equally, because that is how grace works. Any grumbling about that fact means that the complainers, in this case the Jewish community, just haven't fully understood God's generosity.

Once again, we have a problem with an anti-Semitic reading of the text. The frequency of this kind of conclusion in our interpretations reveals an important truth: the Christian tradition has been dealing with a caricature of the Jewish faith for almost two thousand years. The idea that God was vengeful and angry back then, in the "Old Testament," but more kind and loving in the "New Testament," is an indicator that we might not have read either. God is depicted as wrathful in some passages of the Hebrew Bible, but in other passages

God's faithful love, deep forgiveness, and abundant compassion are on display. The same is true in the New Testament. Jesus talks about and embodies a God who is love and cares about the birds and flowers and, of course, us. Yet God also is portrayed as killing Ananias and Sapphira for not contributing enough to the church offering, and the Book of Revelation is replete with divine violence and destruction. This reminds us that the Bible is complicated, offers diverse visions and perspectives, and deserves to be taken very seriously. If this isn't a parable elevating Gentiles to equal, if not greater, status over Jews in the Jesus community, then what is it doing?

To discover an alternative interpretation we must, once again, attempt to bracket our assumption and preconceived ideas about the meaning of this parable. You may recall how we saw in the parable of the tenants that God was not the best fit for understanding who the landowner was. This landowner was an *oikodespótēs*, the owner of many lands and estates, not just a single plot. You may also recall the predatory practices that allowed a person to gobble up the land, all the while displacing those who had lived on and worked it for generations. All of that context applies here as well. The connection Israel/Judah experience to the land was not superficial, but deeply rooted in both their understanding of God and their families. This depth can be seen in a story from the Hebrew Bible about a wicked king, Ahab, who wanted to obtain the vineyard of a man named Naboth.

> *And Ahab said to Naboth, "Give me your vineyard, so that I may have it for a vegetable garden, because it is near my house; I will give you a better vineyard for it, or, if it seems good to you, I will give you its value in money." But Naboth said to Ahab, "The Lord forbid that I should give you my ancestral inheritance."*
>
> (1 Kings 21:2-3)

Notice Naboth's response to Ahab. Not even the request of the king, the prospect of a "better" vineyard, or the offer of money could subvert his ancestral bond to that particular piece of land. This was not land that could even be sold. It was on loan, entrusted to Naboth's family. Of course, Ahab was undeterred by Naboth's refusal. He was brought in on trumped-up charges of cursing God and the king, and eventually stoned to death. In the aftermath Ahab confiscated Naboth's vineyard for himself. While set in the ninth century BCE, there are parallels with Jesus's context in the 30s CE. Unjust land grabs were not a thing of the distant past for Jesus's listeners.

VINEYARDS AND COAL MINES

As the story opens, we find ourselves in a vineyard, probably at the time of the harvest. This would have been time-sensitive, urgent work. When the landowner went into the marketplace early (probably around 6 a.m.) looking for workers, he found plenty of them waiting for someone to hire them. He negotiated with some of the workers to come work in his vineyard for the compensation of a denarius for the day's work. A denarius was a Roman coin, one that would have been engraved with the image and titles of Caesar. This is the coin Jesus referenced in his response to the question about taxes and Caesar. Such a coin was the standard pay for a day's work in the first century and would not be considered "generous" compensation. Think of it as minimum wage in the US, which shares a similarity with the denarius in that it is not enough to support a family even at the level of subsistence. When these workers were paid, they didn't clear a denarius, either. Like today they would have had to pay taxes, not to mention any debt they had accrued. It reminds me of growing up in the coal fields of Appalachia and the song "Sixteen Tons" recorded by Tennessee Ernie Ford. The lyrics refer to the amount of coal being mined and the disappointing economic result:

> You load sixteen tons, what do you get?
> Another day older and deeper in debt.

In the case of these vineyard workers, you work your hands, back, and knees to the point of exhaustion and you still don't have enough for daily bread or anything else. The landowner's vineyard, however, must have been doing very well. A few hours later, at 9 a.m., he returned to find more hands to ensure a successful harvest. He found more workers standing around "idle," which is an interesting word to choose. It can imply being at leisure, or laziness. These workers clearly aren't experiencing leisure, are they? To fully translate this, we could say this wealthy landowner went back and saw some more workers standing around, in his mind, being lazy. He recruited them to work his vineyard that day with the assurance that he would pay them "whatever is right." No negotiations, no back-and-forth. There is no union or collective bargaining agreement in place. These workers need to feed their families so they are forced to trust that this landowner is a man of his word and that his compensation will be just and fair.

This same action is repeated at noon and again at three in the afternoon. This harvest was apparently bountiful. Finally, at 5 p.m. he returned one final time to find still others who had not found work for the day. He approached the workers and asked, "Why are you standing here idle all day?" Their response also revealed their vulnerable position: "Because no one has hired us." This is a revealing answer, because it alludes to the reality that those looking for work far outnumbered the jobs available. This allowed the wealthy landowners to depress wages, because these workers had no leverage or bargaining power. If they didn't want to take the job, he could move on to the next worker. The workers themselves had no such guarantee or opportunity.

We must also raise the question, Why wouldn't this landowner save himself the trouble and just hire a sufficient workforce from the get-go? Why hire a few at a time and have to keep coming back looking for more? It is not because he's moved that so many people are needing work so, in great compassion, he keeps coming back and hiring more and more. If that were the case, he could have hired them all at six in the morning. This context implies the exact opposite. This landowner is trying to avoid spending his funds on labor; he's trying to keep his overhead low to maximize his profits, with no consideration for the pressure it places on the lean workforce he already hired. This, friends, is called exploiting your workers.

You can probably understand the viewpoint of, if not empathize with, those hired first when they are compensated the same as those hired right before quitting time. Yes, they grumbled, but wouldn't we? They felt cheated, but wouldn't we? Their very existence was one of vulnerability, hanging by a thread. No doubt this felt like more than an insult. It was an act of economic violence, which, by the way, the landowner didn't have the courage to do himself. He allowed his "manager" to do his dirty work for him.

The landowner responded to their growing criticisms by gaslighting them, calling their complaints invalid and accusing them of being envious of his generosity to others. After all, they had a deal, and he is doing nothing wrong by paying them what was agreed upon. He asserts, in the Greek, that he has acted "lawfully" toward them. That may have been technically true, but we all know that there is a difference between what is legal and what is just. Laws are often geared toward protecting the powerful at the expense of the powerless. Further, he asks the grumbling workers, "Am I not allowed to do what I choose with what belongs to me?" Assuming crowds would not sit silently during a story like this, I imagine this line would have elicited a strong response. Based on the tradition the answer is a resounding *no* because it isn't his; it doesn't belong to him. It was acquired unjustly, as a result of taking advantage of laws that were created to enhance the rich and bleed what little the poor had from them; laws that allow the Ahabs of the world to railroad the Naboths without any consequence.

The language used when the landowner responds to the complaining workers is also important. When he asks, "Or are you envious because I am generous?" he literally says, "Is your eye evil because I am good?" To have an evil eye meant that a person was envious and stingy, while having a "single" or good/healthy eye meant extended goodwill and generosity toward others. The irony is this landowner is not really being generous, both in the amount he paid any of the workers or the way he distributed the pay.

Finally, the result of the landowner's manipulation could ultimately end up pitting the workers against one another. Imagine how those who labored all day in the scorching sun felt watching those who just arrived being compensated the same amount. They couldn't do anything about the landowner, due to the monumental power differential. If they tried going on strike, he'd just go get other workers. Day laborers weren't in the category known as the "expendables" for no reason. The harvest was plentiful, but so was the mass of people looking for employment. They could, however, blame these other workers who showed up late and got the same pay. After all, they might have wondered, would the landowner have paid us more if they hadn't shown up? Did they take the money out of our pockets and bread out of our children's mouths? In an exploitative economy, those at the top can often get by unscathed, while their employees blame one another for the problem. The real problem isn't the other workers, but the system that perpetuates the injustice and inequality.

The real problem isn't the other workers, but the system that perpetuates the injustice and inequality.

What emerges for me when this story is allowed to be read within the economic situation in which it occurred is a completely different understanding of this parable. This is not a story about a generous God doling out grace like an episode of Oprah's "Favorite Things." (You get a denarius, and you get a denarius and.... You get the picture.) It is instead a story all too familiar to the oppressed, then and now, of how the wealthy and powerful exploit loopholes and labor to enrich themselves and their friends.

Why would Jesus tell a story like this? How does it fit into his larger vision of God's kingdom being realized on earth as it is in heaven? To discover that we need only look back one chapter, to Matthew 19.

RICH MEN AND GOD'S KINGDOM

In Matthew 19 we find what is probably a familiar story to many of us, the story of the "rich young ruler." While that is the title we have given to this story, there is no single version of it that describes the character that way. Here in Matthew, he is a rich and young. In Mark, which predates Matthew, he's just a rich man. Finally, in Luke, he's a rich ruler.

A brief sketch of the story is necessary. This rich young man came to Jesus to ask an important question. "What good deed must I do," he asked, "to have eternal life." This is not a question about "going to heaven" or the afterlife. He's asking about how to participate in "the Age to Come," the messianic age when God would put the world right and end injustice and suffering. Jesus used the phrase "kingdom of God" as a shorthand for this idea. After a brief but illuminating back-and-forth Jesus responded by telling him that, if he really wanted to participate in the kingdom of God, then he should sell his possessions, give the money to the poor, and follow Jesus. That is a big ask, isn't it? Why would Jesus take such an approach? Shouldn't he have weaned him a little at a time? Wouldn't it be nice to have a rich guy around to help fund the work?

Possessing wealth in the first century was not a morally neutral act. As we've seen with these landowners, there was a real human cost and impact. This invitation from Jesus was not some test of obedience; it was the only way for this rich young man to experience that for which he claimed to long. Hoarding his wealth was actively preventing the Kingdom from being experienced by his neighbors. If he responded to Jesus's challenge by divesting himself of his wealth, that would concretely and literally make the kingdom of God visible in and for his community. It was just a bridge too far, however. He walked away from Jesus grieving, the text says. He wanted to experience the Kingdom; he just didn't want it to come at the expense of his own comfort. To understand why Jesus told the parable of the workers, we need to look at the conversation between Jesus and his disciples that came as a result of the above interaction.

Then Jesus said to his disciples, "Truly I tell you, it will be hard for a rich person to enter the kingdom of heaven. Again I tell you, it is easier for a camel to go through the eye of a needle than for someone who is rich to enter the kingdom of God." When the disciples heard this, they were greatly astounded and said, "Then who can be saved?" But Jesus looked at them and said, "For mortals it is impossible, but for God all things are possible."

Then Peter said in reply, "Look, we have left everything and followed you. What then will we have?" Jesus said to them, "Truly I tell you, at the renewal of all things, when the Son of Man is seated on the throne of his glory, you who have followed me will also sit on twelve thrones, judging the twelve tribes of Israel. And everyone who has left houses or brothers or sisters or father or mother or wife or children or fields for my name's sake will receive a hundredfold and will inherit eternal life. But many who are first will be last, and the last will be first.

(Matthew 19:23-30)

For our purposes the focus is on Peter's reaction to Jesus's statement about rich people and God's kingdom. Peter pointed out how he and the other disciples have done the very thing Jesus called the rich young man to do. They left everything behind to follow Jesus. For Peter, Andrew, James, and John, that looked like deserted boats and fishing gear. In the case of Matthew, it was an abandoned tax-collection station. How would they fare in the Kingdom to come? There is a tinge of weariness in that question. As Peter and the others watched the rich young man walk away, they had to experience more than a little doubt and frustration. Jesus hadn't sold the man on the Kingdom vision. He walked away with all of this stuff and likely went back to his spacious and well-appointed home for a lavish meal, while Jesus's own disciples had left their houses and lives behind to join the work of bringing the kingdom of God to bear on their present reality. The fatigue had to be creeping in on them.

Jesus responded with a reassurance that their sacrifice and commitment would not be in vain or for naught. They would, in the world made right, also experience the justice and plenty of God's enough-ness. I read in these words an encouragement to keep going, to not give up, and to keep building the Kingdom. But what does this have to do with the parable of the workers in the vineyard?

GOD ISN'T LIKE THAT

Jesus tells this parable right after this interaction with his disciples not as a comparison between the landowner and God, but for the exact opposite reason. It's for the purpose of contrast. When we assign the landowner the role of God in the parable, we end up missing the power of the story. Peter's question is, "What about us?" To which Jesus responds reassuringly, "You know how the world works, but God is not like the rich and powerful of this world. God is not like the landowner."

Like many other parables Jesus told, this story is subversive. The understanding in the ancient world was that the gods were on the side of the rich and powerful, evidenced by the fact that they were rich and powerful. The gods were on the side of those at the top. It's a pretty convenient idea for those who want to maintain the status quo of their control and wealth. In the tradition of the Hebrew Scriptures, however, God is understood to be found among the powerless and oppressed. This God hears the cry of the enslaved Hebrews and brings about their liberation. This God sends the prophets to decry injustice and call the people back toward faithfulness to God, which looks a lot like doing justice and loving neighbors and enemies. In the Jesus story this God works to bring the Kingdom on earth as it is in heaven, not through violence but through nonviolent, generous, and compassionate love. God is not a dictator on an unbridled ego trip. Nor is God best imaged by the metaphor of landowners and vindictive monarchs. For Jesus it seems that God was best understood in the context of community—in the sharing of food, the extending of forgiveness, and the healing embrace of compassion.

For Jesus it seems that God was best understood in the context of community—in the sharing of food, the extending of forgiveness, and the healing embrace of compassion.

Many of us have inherited an image of God in which God is understood to be just as exploitative, vindictive, violent, and cutthroat as the powerful figures in the parables of Jesus. We have imported the values of our culture into the stories and ultimately attached them to the character of God. My hope is that, as we have unraveled the conventional readings of these parables and offered contextually faithful alternatives in their place, we have instilled an awareness and attentiveness around what God is like and how we read the Bible in the light of God's goodness.

EVERYONE GETS A VINE

There are several important connections between this ancient parable and our lives today. The first is a caution. The standard reading of this parable, along with those of the tenants and the wedding party, turns the oppressed into the villains of the story, while letting the actual villains off the hook. It baptizes the actions of predatory landowners and kings out for revenge, while condemning workers who've been cheated and undervalued.

In 2023 an unknown singer/songwriter from Appalachia, named Oliver Anthony, released a song called "Rich Men North of Richmond." It is an angry lament about the way the rich and powerful politicians in Washington, DC, have forgotten places like Appalachia, all the while their wealth and power grow unchecked and protected. It's a reality that people in my home region have always known—unsafe drinking water, few jobs that pay a living wage, and ravaging by the opioid epidemic. However, something that happens in Anthony's song is also something that happens in this parable, and it's important to notice it. At one point in the song, he takes aim at people who receive government assistance, as if they are the enemy or cause of the problems. It's an unfortunate shift and scapegoating of people who just aren't the problem. The problem is the system—how it's set up, who it benefits, and who it hurts. Anthony has the right anger, I think, but he points it in the wrong direction.

This attitude pervades the parable as well in a couple of places. First, we see this attitude in the way the landowner talks about the workers. If you recall, he calls them "idle," which essentially translates to "lazy." They weren't lazy, however. That is clearly indicated in the fact that they came to find work, but there weren't enough jobs to go around. Can't you just hear the wealthy landowner saying to these workers, "If you just worked harder…"? It's a sentiment we hear today, too, and it ignores the systemic issues in place that make a person working two or three jobs for minimum wage unable to feed their families. Blaming workers isn't the solution, but changing the system is. This isn't just a social or economic issue; it is a gospel issue, a kingdom of God issue.

At the time of this writing, a story has been circulating in the news about a fifth grader in Missouri who raised enough money to pay off the lunch debt for students at his school and a high school. All the reports celebrated the compassion and kindness of the student, which they should have. It was a very Jesus-y thing to do. However, shouldn't we also talk about the fact that kids can incur lunch debt at all? Isn't that a big problem, indicative of something deeply wrong within our system?

One of my favorite prophetic visions in the Bible comes from the Book of Micah. In chapter 4 the prophet envisions the age to come, that time of peace and justice for which so many of us long. In this vision the violence with which we have become all too numb to and familiar with will finally end as swords are beaten into plowshares and assault weapons become farming implements. Notice this beautiful, hopeful result of that transformation:

> But they shall all sit under their own vines and under their own fig trees,
> and no one shall make them afraid,
> for the mouth of the LORD of hosts has spoken.
>
> (Micah 4:4)

They shall sit under their own vines and fig trees. Peace, stability, and the enough-ness that are the markers of God's dream for the world fulfilled. I have come to believe that people who have gardens understand God's kingdom better than the rest of us. At least the ones in my life do. Every time I am around them, I go home with a couple bags full of fresh fruit and vegetables—tomatoes, zucchini, squash, corn, onions, various melons, you get the (delicious) picture. They often insist that we take something with us. Their impulse is not to hoard, but to share, and their generosity benefits so many others. In Jesus's vision that is how the kingdom of God works. It is not advanced through adherence to doctrines or dogmas or winning theological arguments. Instead, it comes through the sharing of food and drink, an ever-expanding table with room for all, and the work that we do to make the world a more just and generous place for everyone.

POSTSCRIPT

There is a maxim in communication theory that says, "The medium is the message." It was first coined by a Canadian theorist named Marshall McLuhan and it speaks to the idea that how we choose to communicate something, the medium, impacts what we are communicating, the message. For example, when people communicate something via social media, they might do it in a way that is more confrontational or pointed than they might if they were in conversation face-to-face with someone. The medium, social media, shapes the message by creating a layer of separation between the people doing the communicating.

Another example of this medium-is-the-message idea gets to the very heart of this book. Jesus's medium of choice was story, not lecture. That format is revealing, in that a lecture is generally one-sided, while a story is participatory. Lectures may elicit questions, but stories invite listeners to be part of solutions. A well-crafted story is an invitation to see oneself as part of the action, not just as a spectator. That, I think, was Jesus's whole point all along. We are not props, but actors. We are not meant to blend in, but to shape the future of the narrative.

Throughout this book we have heard stories, for instance, that Jesus told that were all about his vision of the kingdom of God: How does the Kingdom come? How is it received? How does it challenge the status quo? Through parables Jesus invited (and invites) his listeners to grapple with the disjointedness between the reality of lived experience and the possibility of God's dream. According to Jesus, the gap between those two becoming one isn't as wide as we might believe. It begins to close when we open our hearts and minds to align them with practical action in the real world. Parables are not just about what is, but about what can be. I hope that this study sparked your imagination and stirred up hope for what could be if we chose to accept the invitation to join the Kingdom movement.

Parables are not just about what is, but about what can be.

LET'S BE GOOD ANCESTORS

Every July, I drive seven hours to a farm in North Carolina to participate in the Wild Goose Festival. The image of a "wild goose" is one that comes to us from the Celtic tradition. While the Gospels use the image of a dove, with all of the important peacemaking connotations that brings, the Celts chose to also describe the Spirit as wild, untamable, and exciting. That four or five days sweating in the summer heat are probably my favorite of the year.

Last summer I had the good fortune to share the stage with my dear friend Jonah Overton. One of my favorite things about them is how much they share my love of Scripture, and how seriously they take the Bible. A comment they made in a conversation we had about how we read the Bible really stuck with me, and I've been thinking about it ever since. Jonah said, paraphrased, "We spend a lot of time trying to make our ancestors proud, but we should really spend our time trying to be good ancestors that are trying to make our kids and grandkids proud." That, my friends, will preach.

Jesus's parables call us to that vocation of being good ancestors. His stories create a narrative world that exposes the present moment and calls us into the action—to take our place in shaping the future in a more just and generous way. Bringing that future into the present is our calling and our work. It is a difficult task and also a labor of love. To help others see the possibility that is before us we will need new generations of storytellers who can spark both imagination and extend invitation to this work. I think of how my dad would pose a "for instance" to me as a teenager and how I have, even accidentally, continued that tradition with my own son. Perhaps he will do the same for his own kids someday. That is both the beauty and power of stories—they connect us to the past, to the present, and to the future.

In many ways our current context experiences overlap with the world Jesus knew. We are in uncertain days. Many people are afraid of what the future brings. We long for a better, more just world. So did Jesus. His stories from long ago still speak, sometimes hauntingly so, and call us into the work of midwifing into existence the world of which we dream—and that God dreams of too: a present, earthly reality. May we decide to join God in this work. May we do what we can, when we can, and by doing so leave our own mark in the long history of humans collaborating with God to make a better world possible. May we be good ancestors.

NOTES

Introduction

1   John Dominic Crossnan, *The Dark Interval: Towards a Theology of Story* (Niles, IL: Argus Communications, 1975), 56.

Chapter 2

1   Pliny the Elder, *Natural History*, 19.170-171, http://www.perseus.tufts.edu /hopper/text?doc=Perseus:abo:phi,0978,001:19#note-link409.

Chapter 4

1   Federal Reserve. *Distribution of Household Wealth in the U.S. since 1989*, September 20, 2024, https://www.federalreserve.gov/releases/z1/dataviz/dfa/distribute /table/#range:2009.2,2024.2;quarter:139;series:Assets;demographic:networth ;population:1,9;units:shares.

Watch videos based on *Parables: Putting Jesus's Stories in their Place* with Josh Scott through Amplify Media.

Amplify Media is a multimedia platform that delivers high quality, searchable content with an emphasis on Wesleyan perspectives for churchwide, group, or individual use on any device at any time. In a world of sometimes overwhelming choices, Amplify gives church leaders and congregants media capabilities that are contemporary, relevant, effective, and, most importantly, affordable and sustainable. With *Amplify Media* church leaders can:

+ Provide a reliable source of Christian content through a Wesleyan lens for teaching, training, and inspiration in a customizable library
+ Deliver their own preaching and worship content in a way the congregation knows and appreciates
+ Build the church's capacity to innovate with engaging content and accessible technology
+ Equip the congregation to better understand the Bible and its application
+ Deepen discipleship beyond the church walls